# Continuing the Journey: Cultivating Lived Faith
## by
## Julie Dienno-Demarest

© 2014

ISBN 9-781500-474591

# Dedication

For my boys:
my husband, Peter
and my sons, Alex and Max

# Table of Contents

# Abbreviations

# Introduction

Continuing the Journey is about cultivating a lived faith. It is one thing to know about your faith; it is another to actually put insights into action and live as a disciple of Christ. Likewise, it is one thing to go through the motions; it is another to understand why we do what we do. Each chapter will help you cultivate lived faith by asking you to reflect on your life, bring it into conversation with your faith, and specifically challenge you to invite the transforming power of the Holy Spirit into your life by expressing a commitment to act.

Lived faith—and the process of transformation—is neither easy nor automatic. Rather, it is a lifelong journey that requires personal commitment.

Perhaps you are committed to the path of discipleship. Perhaps you were raised in the faith, but have been struggling. Perhaps you find yourself in the place of earnest searching, aware of more questions than answers. Wherever you find yourself along this journey, this book is for you.

I come to writing this book with a background as a religious educator. I do not write to try to convince you. I write to help facilitate your understanding of the faith, prompt your reflection, and encourage you along your journey.

Whether I was teaching high school or writing curriculum materials for a textbook series, I would occasionally discuss the topics I was working on with other adults—some committed faithful, others struggling in their faith. I was continually surprised by how many adults remarked, "Wow, I need to take a class like that." It's not that everyone I talked to was uneducated in their faith; it's that most hadn't thought about certain aspects of their faith as it related to their life today.

In the first chapter, you will be asked a series of questions intended to help you unpack your intentions and your starting point. In the chapters that follow, we will discuss an aspect of faith in a way that is both accessible and engaging. Throughout the book, you will find questions for reflection. It is in these reflection questions that you will be invited to bring your faith into conversation with your life. Take the time to be as honest as you can. Skip the questions that don't speak to your heart at this time. This process is for you; you will not be graded.

To help you continue on your journey—to help you bring about the changes you want to see in your life—each chapter will offer *information*, invite *formation*, and encourage *transformation*. The information is intended to increase your understanding about different aspects of our faith. With formation, I will prompt you to reflect on your life experiences, in hopes that you will allow your heart to be affected by what you learn. When we bring our lives into conversation with our faith, when we put the insights into practice, we grow in faith and our lives are transformed. Transformation is not something that "happens to us," nor is it something we achieve on our own. Rather, transformation happens when we accept the invitation to cooperate with God's grace.

Whether you choose to read *Continuing the Journey* in a group (book-club discussion) or independently, I encourage you to read at a pace that honors the time for reflection. With 28 chapters, you can read a chapter-a-day for a month, or just choose a couple chapters per week. Within each chapter, the questions are numbered for easy reference within a group discussion.

In *Continuing the Journey*, as I present a variety of theological topics, I will cite references from Scripture and Tradition, particularly from *The Catechism of the Catholic Church*. Any references from Scripture will refer to the translation that is used in Mass: the New American Bible Revised Edition (NABRE), unless otherwise indicated.

Rather than using footnotes or endnotes to cite Church documents, I will indicate a reference by using a standard abbreviation and paragraph number, such as (CCC, 309) or (*LG* 16). Just like Scripture is broken down into Books, Chapters, and Verses, Church documents—including the *Catechism*—are broken down into paragraph numbers. Sometimes a number can have multiple "paragraphs," which can make it somewhat confusing. Thus, you may hear them referred to as sections, articles, numbers, or paragraphs. And just like Scripture, there are also standard abbreviations for documents themselves, such as *LG* for *Lumen Gentium* or CCC for *The Catechism of the Catholic Church* (see the Abbreviations page).

Every Church document that I will reference (including the *Catechism*) is available online, free of charge, either through the United States Conference of Catholic Bishops (USCCB) website (www.usccb.org) or the Vatican (www.vatican.va) or both. My hope is that you feel encouraged and empowered to visit these sites to read and learn more about your faith.

By way of gratitude, I want to thank the ACTS Retreat Community at St. Paul the Apostle Catholic Church in Houston, Texas for their desire to live their faith. It was this desire that prompted me to write this book. I thank Heidi Clark, St. Paul's Director of Adult Ministry and the ACTS Core Team for their excitement and encouragement for this project. I thank my ACTS Sisters, my friends, my mother, Maureen Dienno, and my sister, Laurie Dienno Pharr for reading, responding, reflecting, and cheering me on throughout the process of writing. It is with profound gratitude that I thank my extraordinary husband, Peter Demarest, for his patience, love, support, encouragement, co-parenting, editing, and marketing.

Peace be with you as you continue your journey.

# Chapter 1

# Me, Here, Now

*I am a do-er. Sometimes when I am able to stop all the "doing" and simply "be" in the present moment, I'll take a picture of my view. Not a "selfie" (self-portrait), but rather a picture of my view that includes my feet, such as on the beach or in the hammock… I call it "Me. Here. Now." In these moments, I stop. I am aware. And I am intentionally present. This is a significant step for me because I am always on the go. Who am I, right here, right now? Me, Here, Now: I am a perfectionist that is trying to redefine what it means to be perfect. For me, now, "perfect" means letting go of whatever I need to let go of so that I can be a loving presence to those who matter most to me. I am a mother of two elementary school-aged boys striving to live out my faith, as best I can in my life right now.*

~~~~~

Consider your starting point here, at this moment, as you read this book. Are you committed in your faith and looking to learn and grow? Are you unsure about your faith, perhaps having more questions than answers?

1. What is your "Me-Here-Now" starting point? What recent experiences have had the greatest impact on your faith?

2.  What are you struggling with, right now?

3.  As you consider bringing your life into conversation with your faith, what questions come up for you?  What concerns (or fears) do you have?

4.  What do you feel God calling you to do next?   What are the next steps you are going to take?

As you consider who and where you are at this moment – and what brings you to the point of reading this book – recall the story of the Transfiguration:

> Jesus took Peter, John, and James and went up the mountain to pray. While he was praying his face changed in appearance and his clothing became dazzling white. And behold, two men were conversing with him, Moses and Elijah, who appeared in glory and spoke of his exodus that he was going to accomplish in Jerusalem. Peter and his companions had been overcome by sleep, but becoming fully awake, they saw his glory and the two men standing with him. As they were about to part from him, Peter said to Jesus, "Master, it is good that we are here; let us make three tents, one for you, one for Moses, and one for Elijah." But he did not know what he was saying. While he was still speaking, a cloud came and cast a shadow over them, and they became frightened when they entered the cloud. Then from the cloud came a voice that said, "This is my chosen Son; listen to him." After the voice had spoken, Jesus was found alone. They fell silent and did not at that time tell anyone what they had seen. (Luke 9:28-36)

When we read the story of the transfiguration, our focus is drawn to Jesus. Take a closer look at the actions and words of Peter, John, and James. After being overcome by sleep, they awoke to the glory of God. Peter's instinct was to pitch a tent and stay there, but that wasn't the intent. They were called to share in an amazing experience. As they fell silent and didn't talk about the details of their experience, we can rest assured that they, themselves, were changed by seeing Jesus in this new way.

When an amazing experience awakes us to the glory of God we may find ourselves wanting to stay exactly where we are. Like Peter, we may want to pitch a tent on the mountaintop. But we, too, must go on.

~~~~~

*In the eulogy for his wife's funeral, Brian spoke of the desire to pitch a tent. Amalour had an unending quest for improvement. In their marriage—in their lives—they'd do the work and come to a plateau. It was a nice plateau, on which Brian was ready to pitch a tent and enjoy the view. And Amalour would say no; we're not there yet. We can do better than this. There's more to see; there's more to do. Again, and again, and again in their lives, Amalour was always striving for something more… for something better… in all the ways that mattered.*

~~~~~

An experience might very well change us, but only if we're willing to forgo pitching a tent. We must come down from the mountain and make it happen. The most effective changes you can make begin within your own heart. As you read this book, the hope is that you will integrate new insights as you grow in your faith.

5.  Have you ever had that desire to "pitch a tent"?  Explain.

6.  As you look back on your life, what have been the most significant moments of change?  What changes have you noticed within yourself?  What changes would you like to make?

# Chapter 2

# (Re)Kindling Our Passion for God

One of the most amazing things that happens on a retreat is how excited people get about their faith. In a word, that's evangelization.

1. Before reading any further in this chapter, what comes to mind when you hear the word "evangelization"?

For the longest time, when I'd hear "evangelization," I'd crinkle my nose, thinking it meant proselytizing. I knew my Church, my faith, my God "called" me to do this thing called evangelization, but to be quite honest, I'd really rather not. The problem with this kind of attitude is that the popes, beginning with Pope Paul VI, then Saint John Paul II, then Pope Benedict XVI, and now Pope Francis keep writing and preaching about the "new evangelization." Not only was this "evangelization" thing not going away, each of these popes keep renewing our call to do it.[1]

As it turns out, my understanding of *evangelization* was off—way off—well, kind of off.

---

[1] The continuity in the call for evangelization is worth noting. Pope Paul VI wrote *Evangelii Nuntiandi* (On Evangelization in the Modern World) in 1975, which was the first Church document devoted entirely to the topic of evangelization. Saint John Paul II renewed that call throughout his papacy, particularly in *Redemptoris Missio* (Mission of the Redeemer), 1990, in which he alluded to what is called the "new evangelization," but did not use that phrase. Pope Benedict XVI explicitly referenced the "new evangelization" in a 2010 homily and established the Pontifical Council for the Promotion of the New Evangelization in that same year. Pope Francis focused on evangelization in his first Apostolic Exhortation *Evangelii Gaudium* (Joy of the Gospel) in 2013. For more about this continuity and the call to evangelization, visit the United States Catholic Bishops website http://www.usccb.org/beliefs-and-teachings/how-we-teach/new-evangelization/disciples-called-to-witness/index.cfm.

## Background

Let's start with a better understanding of evangelization; a definition which honors the intention, style, and practice of the apostles: ***Evangelization is about kindling the burning desire for God in our hearts.***

2.  What kindles the burning desire for God in your heart?  What gets you excited and passionate about your faith?

From the beginning, evangelization meant bringing the Good News of the Gospel to every corner of the earth.  The call to do this is in Scripture (at the very end of the Gospel of Matthew), and we call it "The Great Commission."

> Now the eleven disciples went to Galilee, to the mountain to which Jesus had directed them. When they saw him, they worshiped him; but some doubted. And Jesus came and said to them, "All authority in heaven and on earth has been given to me. Go therefore and make disciples of all nations, baptizing them in the name of the Father and of the Son and of the Holy Spirit, and teaching them to obey everything that I have commanded you. And remember, I am with you always, to the end of the age." (Matthew 28:16-20)

Historically, we have limited our understanding of evangelization to the missionary work of bringing the Good News to people who have never before heard it.  Which, in itself, is fine (if those who are evangelizing are sharing *what* Jesus taught, *how* he taught it: with love, and without force).

However, evangelization was never meant to be equated with the forceful, negative, judgmental practice of proselytizing.  Because, as you may know, that's not how Jesus did things.

Evangelization is about kindling the burning desire for God in our hearts.  Proselytizing is focused on the surface experience of getting someone to agree with you that your religion, belief, or opinion is the right one.  We are not called to proselytize.  We are called to evangelize.

## Renewed Understanding

As we have renewed our understanding for *what* evangelization is—kindling the burning desire for God in our hearts—the Church has also renewed her understanding that we need to evangelize to different people with different "kindling" needs.

There are three distinct groups in need of evangelization:[2]

- **Never Before** – those who have never before heard the Good News

- **Once More** – those who are regular, committed faithful who are in need of rekindling their passion for God. For many, the fire is there, but it wanes. For others, it's less of a fire and more of a flame.

- **This Time with Feeling** – those who (for whatever reason) have left the Church and are "searching" for something… are considering coming back… are unsure… and are in need of kindling that passion, as well as direction, education, healing, etc.

3. Each of us falls somewhere within this range of "kindling needs." Where on this continuum—never before, once more, this time with feeling—would you place yourself? Explain.

## The Circular Cycle

The mission of the Church is to evangelize (to all three groups). There are two important things to notice about that statement.

---

[2] In *Evangelli Nuntiandi*, Pope Paul VI identified two groups in need of evangelization: *ad gentes* (Latin for "to the world") as well as those who are baptized but no longer practice their faith. The "three distinct groups" are referenced in *Redemptoris Missio*, 33 as well as in *The General Directory for Catechesis*, 58. The phrase "the new evangelization" specifically refers to reaching out to people in the third group. I wish to acknowledge two professors from my 2001-2002 graduate studies at Boston College for the "never before, once more, and this time with feeling" labels: Michael Horan and Jane Regan.

First, "the Church" is not a building or an organization; it is not a "they" or "them." *We* are the Church. *We* are the Body of Christ. So this evangelizing mission is *our* mission. *We* are called to evangelize.

Second, the best thing about the mission to be evangelizing is that it's quite a circular cycle. When you kindle your own passion for God, it has a tendency to bubble over to others.

Think about those who have just attended a retreat. Chances are that retreat experience was incredibly evangelizing. When retreatants return home, they are filled with the Holy Spirit, and there's a pretty good chance that they can't help but share their joy. In doing so, they went from being evangelized (by other members of the Church) to evangelizing others. That's the beautiful circular design of evangelization.

What I love most about this renewed understanding of evangelization is that there are *many, many* legitimate ways to evangelize.

Start with yourself. Ask yourself: **What fuels my own passion for God?** And then, (presuming it is life-giving and loving) do that thing. Here's a list of ideas (be sure to check out your Parish Bulletin for specific opportunities):

- Go do service (visit the sick or elderly, help the homeless, build homes at Habitat for Humanity)
- Participate in Mass (sing, read, serve, pray, adore)
- Learn about your faith – see what classes or book studies you could participate in
- Spend time being intentionally present to your friends, family, children, siblings, and parents. Nurture relationships.
- Do the thing God called you to do–that thing that fills your heart–and praise God for joy
- Attend (or team for) a retreat
- Spend time in nature, thanking God for the gift of Creation

When you tend to the fire within your own heart, your passion for God spills out into the hearts of others. One of the most important ways that this happens is by being a *wordless witness* of Christian faith to people you encounter on a daily basis.[3]

---

[3] The popular expression "Preach the Gospel at all times; use words when necessary" is widely attributed to St. Francis of Asissi, but he never actually said it. Instead, I use the phrase *wordless witness* because it was used by Pope Paul VI in *Evangelli Nuntiandi*. In paragraph 21, Pope Paul VI discusses the importance of being a witness of the Christian faith by the witness of our life: "Above all the Gospel must be proclaimed by witness. Take a Christian or a handful of Christians who, in the midst of their own community, show their capacity for understanding and acceptance, their sharing of life and destiny with other people, their solidarity with the efforts of all for whatever is noble and good. Let us suppose that, in addition, they radiate in an altogether simple and unaffected way their faith in values that go beyond current values, and their hope in something that is not seen and that one would not dare to imagine. Through this wordless witness these Christians stir up irresistible questions in the hearts of those who see how they live: Why are

Of course, evangelization also includes a willingness to talk about your faith with others. As St. Peter said,

> Always be ready to give an explanation to anyone who asks you for a reason for your hope, but do it with gentleness and reverence, keeping your conscience clear. (1 Peter 3:15)

Many of us hesitate at the idea of evangelizing through words for fear of proselytizing. Yet, so often this is simply a matter of being willing to answer someone's questions to the best of your ability.

~~~~~

*I was watching my friend's eight-year-old daughter a few days after my son's First Communion party, and she asked me some questions about the significance of the event. She knew it was special—a celebration was involved—but wondered what exactly it was, especially since her family was not Catholic. My answer was brief, age appropriate, and respectful.*

*"In the Bible, we read that Jesus shared himself through bread and wine. At our Church, when we share bread and wine, we believe that we are actually, really receiving Jesus."*

*"So Alex was doing that for the very first time. Wow! Is that something I could do?"*

*"Well, it's something we take very seriously, so Alex has been taking classes this past year to really learn about what the Eucharist—which is what we call communion—means. But yes, if you wanted to, you could do that too."*

~~~~~

These are the kinds of conversations that we are most likely to have throughout our daily lives; casual conversations that gently and reverently explain the reason for our hope.

4. What kind of questions about your faith have you been asked? How have you responded?

---

they like this? Why do they live in this way? What or who is it that inspires them? Why are they in our midst? Such a witness is already a silent proclamation of the Good News and a very powerful and effective one...All Christians are called to this witness, and in this way they can be real evangelizers."

5. What do you currently do to participate in the evangelizing mission of the Church? (Remember that means both: how are you kindling your own passion for God and how are you spreading that to others?)

6. Is there something more that you feel God prompting you to do to participate in the evangelizing mission of the Church? What are the next steps you will take?

# Chapter 3

# Mistaking Spiritual Perfectionism for Discipleship

1. If there was one thing you could (magically, effortlessly) change about yourself, what would it be?




   Play along: come up with one thing.  Perhaps it's...
   - developing a virtuous habits (and eliminating unhealthy ones)
   - addressing some physical characteristic (in the realm of body image or ability)
   - acquiring a desired talent



2. Sit with your answer.  What does it tell you about yourself?  Is it just for fun? Does it have to do with something you struggle with?  How does it relate to your personal goals? Hopes? Dreams? Most importantly: What does it tell you about where you are on the spectrum between self-love and self-loathing?

In the lifelong journey of growth and change, there is usually some *thing* or another that we are working on improving. This is good. After all, we are Christians on the path of discipleship.

What does discipleship mean? Contemporary Christians tend to use the terms apostle and disciple interchangeably, but there is an important distinction. The "twelve" (plus St. Paul) are the apostles who were called by Jesus. But many more—men and women—felt called to follow him. They listened. They learned. They changed their paths in life because of him. These followers weren't just believers; they were disciples. These disciples were informed, formed, and transformed by Jesus. Believers intellectually accept what Jesus taught. Disciples take his message to heart and their lives are transformed.

So getting back to that *thing* we are working on improving: as Christians on the path of discipleship, we are called to "conversion" – to turn away from sin and be faithful to the Gospel. However, there is a legitimate concern for our spiritual well-being insomuch as how we treat ourselves in the process.

You are a child of God, created in God's image and likeness.

> Then God said: Let us make human beings in our image, after our likeness. Let them have dominion over the fish of the sea, the birds of the air, the tame animals, all the wild animals, and all the creatures that crawl on the earth. God created humankind in his image; in the image of God he created them; male and female he created them. (Genesis 1:26-27)

Catholic tradition calls this dynamic sense of value and worth *human dignity*; respect for human dignity is at the root of one's own healthy self-love, and it's the basis for morality and social justice (See CCC, 1700-1715). Healthy self-love appreciates the goodness that is present within each person.

3. When it comes to the things about yourself that you want to change, do you honor the image of God within? Do you treat yourself with the love and respect that the image of God deserves?

Several years ago, I started painting as a hobby. At the beginning I was really intimidated by the permanence of painting on canvas, until a friend said quite simply: if I didn't like something, I could *just paint over it*.

How freeing! This insight allowed me to experiment without hesitation. I had infinite do-over's. If something didn't work, I could just try again, and again, and again until I liked it. Sometimes that meant starting over. Sometimes it meant painting over the one spot that wasn't working. It removed the pressure of feeling like I had to have the whole thing perfectly planned out before I even started. Or feeling like it was ruined by one little (or big) mistake.

What a wonderful approach to all of life! *If you don't like something, just paint over it.* As I looked around at my house, my relationships, my work, and inward at myself, this insight became one of *transformation.* Don't trash it; don't brush it under the carpet and ignore it. If I didn't like something, I could *transform it.* The very idea of transformation cultivates hope.

In faith, this is the transformation that is linked to forgiveness. The Greek word for what happens in the transforming process of forgiveness is *metanoia* [pronounced META-NOY-AH]. The literal translation is "a change of heart." *Metanoia* refers to a conversion where the person turns away from what is destructive, hurtful, hateful, and instead turns towards God.

Turning towards God involves

- forgiving oneself and transforming one's own character
- forgiving others, seeking forgiveness from others, and transforming relationships
- seeking forgiveness from God and becoming transformed—a changed person.

Put another way, *metanoia* is about

- becoming more (and more and more) of a good person
- doing what is right
- acting with love
- helping others

4. Looking around your own life, what would you like to "just paint over" and transform?

Too often, however, we can be overly critical of ourselves in a way which is neither helpful nor loving. There is a fine line between *goals that motivate* and the expectation of *nothing less than perfection that can shut a person down.*

5. Do you tend to have more "goals that motivate" or an expectation of "nothing less than perfection"? How does that impact your spiritual journey?

**The Need for Perfection**

There are two times that the word "perfect" appears in the Gospels, both in the Gospel According to Matthew. The first is in Matthew 5:48, which is the part of the Sermon on the Mount in which Jesus discusses *Love of Enemies.*

> You have heard that it was said, "You shall love your neighbor and hate your enemy." But I say to you, love your enemies, and pray for those who persecute you, that you may be children of your heavenly Father, for he makes his sun rise on the bad and the good, and causes rain to fall on the just and the unjust. For if you love those who love you, what recompense will you have? Do not the tax collectors do the same? And if you greet your brothers only, what is unusual about that? Do not the pagans do the same? So be perfect, just as your heavenly Father is perfect. (Matthew 5:43-48)

The second appears in Matthew 19:21 within the story of *The Rich Young Man.*

> Now someone approached him and said, "Teacher, what good must I do to gain eternal life?" He answered him, "Why do you ask me about the good? There is only One who is good. If you wish to enter into life, keep the commandments." He asked him, "Which ones?" And Jesus replied, "'You shall not kill; you shall not commit adultery; you shall not steal; you shall not bear false witness; honor your father and your mother'; and 'you shall love your neighbor as yourself.'" The young man said to him, "All of these I have observed. What do I still lack?" Jesus said to him, "If you wish to be perfect, go, sell what you have and give to the poor, and you will have treasure in heaven. Then come, follow me." When the young man heard this statement, he went away sad, for he had many possessions. (Matthew 19:16-22)

MISTAKING SPIRITUAL PERFECTIONISM FOR DISCIPLESHIP ⅄ 15

## If You Wish to Be Perfect...

In reality, there is always room for improvement. If we think we are all done with the personal/spiritual growth thing (as if to say: "*I have arrived*"), we are reminded that our work is never complete. It is then that Jesus will say to us, *if you wish to be perfect...*

It's the all-or-nothing extremes that are useless. Unhelpful. Paralyzing. In no way does Jesus insinuate that this rigid interpretation of perfection is what we are to aim for.

Growth—change—is a process. *Metanoia* is a "turning" *away from* something (sinful) and *towards* God (who is wholeness, life, and truth).

6. Think about the self-improvement or "areas of growth" that you are working on in your life. Do you treat yourself with love in the process of turning? Or do you become overly critical and hateful about perceived failures?

To move beyond my own struggle with perfectionism, I found it helpful to redefine "perfect" as *functioning at my best, right now.* For me that implies being my best and doing my best in the present moment, while looking to take the next step to become better.

The "next step" is an important concept in overcoming paralyzing perfectionism, because it recognizes the space between the "reality of now" and the "ideal" or "goal." And in order for it to *function*, the "next step" should be realistic. Small. Doable. And then after each step is accomplished, celebrate the success. And build upon it. Because *that* is perfect.

7. In what way have you struggled with perfectionism? What successes have you had with true conversion or metanoia?

8. What are the "next steps" you feel called to make on your path of discipleship?

# Chapter 4

# Heaven, Hell, Purgatory and Judgment

As a child, I absolutely loved the 1960's Disney movie *Pollyanna* with Hayley Mills. There was something about the hope and joy that this little girl brought into the life of so many people that spoke to my heart. One of the bits of dialogue that always stuck with me had to do with the message about "glad" and "sad" pieces of Scripture.

Pollyanna innocently and gently mentions to the Reverend–whose weekly sermons had been filled with fire and brimstone–how her father had noted over 800 verses in the Bible in which God tells us to rejoice or be glad or be happy. If the Lord took the trouble to tell us 800 times that he wants us to rejoice, then He must really mean it.

These days, to accuse someone of being "a Pollyanna" implies being naively optimistic. But I think she was on to something. An inordinate focus on the fire and brimstone messages of Scripture does damage, scaring people's faith with a paralyzing fear of God and the threat of hell. Many are left wondering: *If God is all loving and forgiving, then how can there be anyone in hell?*

1. How does your own understanding of heaven, hell, and judgment impact your faith? Does it inspire you or fill you with fear? Does it offer hope or leave you with questions?

2. When it comes to the topic of heaven, hell, and judgment, what do you wonder about?

**Imagery**

Most people's understanding of how heaven, hell, and judgment work is a "cartoonized" version of the following:

> Upon death, we imagine standing before the pearly gates. St. Peter looks at the big thick book on his podium. All of the good and all of the bad we have ever done is weighed on some cosmic scale; whichever way the scale tips determines our destiny. If the scale tips "good," then the pearly gates open, choirs of angels sing, and we enter heaven. If the scale tips "bad," then the trap door opens beneath our feet and we descend down to the fiery pits of hell.

That simplistic imagery might work for comic strips, but it is lousy theology and everyone knows it. So why is it so pervasive? From a religious education perspective, these images are easy to visualize, so it engages our *religious imagination*, even if it's unhealthy. The phrase "religious imagination" refers to what happens when we visualize the sacred; it helps us understand meaning beyond what we can express (or comprehend) in words. Our faith is enriched when the substance of Church teaching is able to work its way into the meaning-making of our religious imagination.

So before exploring the language of good theology, consider engaging your religious imagination with healthier imagery:

> Upon the moment of your death, imagine you walk in to an IMAX theatre equipped with a great big sofa in the middle of the room. Who is sitting on this sofa? None other than the Almighty and Ever-Loving God. You take a seat next to the Divine Presence, and God puts His Divine arm around your shoulder. The lights dim, and the instant the movie starts, you immediately recognize it as the story of your life. As it plays, you notice that for every good you have done, God squeezes your arm and lovingly whispers *Thank you!* For all the harmful or hurtful things you said or did… all times you should have done something but didn't… you notice a tear roll down His Divine face. You realize that your thoughts, words, actions, and inactions have *hurt God*. You. Have. Hurt. God. Notice how that realization feels.

> As the movie of your life continues, you also notice that any of those instances that you have expressed sincere remorse for—the ones you have sought forgiveness for in the Sacrament of Reconciliation—do not make it in to the movie, as if God does not feel the need to rehash it.

> The movie ends, the lights come up, God turns to look at you and you realize you are now faced with a choice.

- You can look into God's loving eyes, take responsibility, apologize, and seek forgiveness… to which God will reply, *"Child, you are already forgiven. Welcome home!"*

- Or you can refuse to accept the Truth of what you have made of your life. You can rationalize, make excuses and justify your behavior. You can simply get up and walk out, choosing to believe your own version of events, indifferent to God. In effect, you can reject God and, in doing so, choose hell.

3. What stands out for you in this imagery? What do you find helpful? What questions does it evoke?

## Heaven

God wants heaven for us. God *wants* us to choose heaven. Rather than thinking of heaven as some playground in the sky, think of heaven as *being in the complete and total presence of God*. United with God in heaven is the fulfillment of all longing – of our deepest desires. This is the *beatific vision*–seeing God's face. This joy *is* paradise! A wedding feast! (See CCC, 1023-1029.)

But God is God. And Truth is Truth. And we must choose: God's Truth or your own version of truth. As C.S. Lewis said in *The Great Divorce:*

> There are only two kinds of people in the end: those who say to God, 'Thy will be done,' and those to whom God says, in the end, "Thy will be done."[4]

## Hell

It is in rejecting God and God's Truth that a person *chooses* hell. If heaven is being completely and fully in God's presence, hell is complete isolation from God (see CCC, 1033-1037). We have no idea what complete isolation from God is like. Our lives are

---

[4] C.S. Lewis. *The Great Divorce*. (Macmillan Publishing Company), 1946, 72.

imbued with the presence of God. The grace of the Holy Spirit permeates our lives so much so that we don't even have a concept of what *complete isolation from God* really means.

> They will throw them into the fiery furnace, where there will be wailing and grinding of teeth. (Matthew 13:42)

The images of heaven and hell in Scripture reflect the ancient Israelites methods of conjuring relatable ideas, which are not necessarily literal descriptions. Think about the image of "a fiery furnace."

~~~~~

*Have you ever been badly burned—physically? My sister has. She spent two weeks in the pediatric unit of the burn center of New Jersey when she was 10. Every day burn patients would need to spend time in the "tank room" where the raw skin in their wounds is scrubbed clean of debris to prevent infection; it's more painful than most of us can imagine. A fiery furnace where clothing melts into skin and has to be scrubbed off… Isolation from God feels like that.*

~~~~~

## Purgatory

What if you are the sort of person who needs time to process the difficult truths you faced? You want to take responsibility, you just need time to think and come to terms with things. This is where purgatory comes in. Purgatory is most emphatically *not* a punishment (see CCC, 1031), but rather Church Tradition calls it a time of purification.

To use some traditional vocabulary terms, the explanation thus far has described what Church Tradition refers to as "particular judgment," or when each individual person is judged upon death (CCC, 1021); their immortal soul will go to either heaven, hell or purgatory (CCC, 1022). Ultimately, there will come a time for all decisions to be made… the process of purification will need to be completed at some point; purgatory is not an eternal option. This is what we know as the "last judgment" – the Second Coming at the end of time (CCC 1038-1041).[5]

---

[5] The theological term for this area of study is "eschatology," [pronounced es-ka-tol-oh-gee] which literally means the study of the "last" things. In addition to judgment, heaven, hell, and purgatory, eschatology also includes topics such as the resurrection of the body, the coming of Jesus on the last day, etc. A discussion on eschatology usually prompts two related questions, both of which have to do with the Church's teaching on salvation (or who will be saved). The first concerns the understanding that *salvation is through Christ alone* – an understanding that comes from Scripture: "I am the way and the truth and the life. No one comes to the Father except through me" (John 14:6). The second concerns a teaching that dates back to the 3rd Century: *outside the Church there is no salvation* (CCC, 846). Both of these teachings prompt many to ask: Does this mean that non-Christians are going to hell? In two words, the answer is: not exactly. At the Second Vatican Council (1962-1965), the Church explicitly clarified the teaching on this matter. The *Catechism of the Catholic Church* quotes *Lumen Gentium* (The Dogmatic Constitution of the

4.  How do you respond when someone confronts you with a difficult truth?

5.  What wisdom can you take from the Church's teaching on heaven, hell, and purgatory for your own life?  Is there something that speaks to your heart?  Has something shifted in your understanding?

6.  Is there something you feel called to do differently?  What are the next steps you will take?

---

Church) as it explains: "Those who, through no fault of their own, do not know the Gospel of Christ or his Church, but who nevertheless seek God with a sincere heart, and, moved by grace, try in their actions to do his will as they know it through the dictates of their conscience – those too may achieve eternal salvation" (CCC, 847, *LG* 16).  We may not necessarily understand *how* non-Christians are saved through Christ, but we certainly do believe that their salvation is possible.

# Chapter 5

# What Exactly is the Virtue of Faith

*I met Peter through a friend of a friend at a party, before heading out to see some bands play at a music festival. I was attracted to the trifecta of cute, smart, and funny that he had going on. As we got to know each other, I was shocked to find out that a month before we met, he had run a marathon and completed a 50 mile bike race, and he was about to do a triathlon. He had an average-guy build—a little bit of a beer belly—and didn't look like an athlete; I could not fathom how he could possibly do those things.*

*More than my unhelpful preconceived notions of what an athlete looks like, I had sized up the end-result of all his training efforts as impossible: there is no way I could run a 26.2 mile marathon, no less do all that a triathlon involved: swim 1/2 mile, then bike 12 miles, then run 3 miles. Just no.*

*I saw athleticism as "haves-and-havenots" (and I was a havenot). Like a light switch: it was either on or off, but no in-between.*

*But Peter didn't see what I saw. He saw a training schedule. He saw daily steps along a path. He saw incremental progress building up until he could confidently complete something amazing. Peter's way of seeing things inspired me. He was a regular guy that did a marathon and a triathlon; if he could do it, I could do it. So I did.*

*The following year, I completed my first Danskin Triathlon — an all-women's series that cultivates an environment of encouragement. The swim went okay—though I'm a strong swimmer, I was ill-prepared for fifteen pairs of feet in my face. Towards the end of the 12 mile bike ride, I faced what felt like the largest hill I had ever seen. I wasn't even halfway up, and I was ready to dismount and walk to the top. But in front of me were two plump, middle-aged women, ever-so-slowly biking up-up-up, and encouraging every single person around them. Not only were they not giving up, but they weren't letting anyone else give up either. "You go girl! You got this!" Once their words of support and love reached me, I firmed my resolve to just keep pedaling. Tears welled as I shouted to these women "You two are amazing! Thank you! YOU GO!!" And I was off, finishing the bike and then the run.*

*The back of the medal that each woman receives upon crossing the finish line sums up my experience with profound truth: "The woman who starts the race is not the same woman who finishes the race."*

~~~~~

1.  What are some of the areas in your life that you might have had unhelpful preconceived notions?

**Virtue**

Preconceived notions can be unhelpful and damaging in the world of religious education, particularly that *haves and havenots* mentality when it comes to the topic of virtue. If you look up the definition of virtue, you can see why many people approach it as a light switch, either on or off, but no in-between. The Merriam Webster Dictionary defines virtue as "morally good behavior or character."[6]

The problem is that this leads to a prevailing, yet faulty logic:

*Virtue means morally good behavior.*
*I don't always behave morally.*
*Therefore, I am not virtuous.*

It's not that the folks at Merriam Webster got the definition *wrong*, rather, I just think there's a much more helpful way of thinking about virtue: **Virtue is like a good habit that we can become better at doing.**

Instead of thinking about virtue as *haves and havenots*, try thinking about virtue as a muscle that gets stronger (or weaker). Developing virtue is like training for a race; it's about practicing these good habits over the course of time. When we want to form a good habit—or break a bad habit—we take incremental steps towards a goal.

When you think of virtue, imagine a gradation or a continuum of stronger-to-weaker. See a training schedule. See daily steps along a path. See incremental progress building up until you can confidently complete something amazing. Think of saints and the lives of people who inspire you. [Image 1]

Weaker · Stronger

---

[6] http://www.merriam-webster.com/dictionary/virtue Accessed May 20, 2014.

2. Recall a time when you were making a change—or trying to improve at something. What helped you practice good habits? How did you overcome bad habits?

**The Virtue of Faith**

Traditionally, a discussion of virtue touches upon the four cardinal virtues (prudence, justice, fortitude, and temperance) and three theological virtues (faith, hope, and love). Of these seven virtues, faith seems to be the one people have the most unhelpful preconceived notions about.

> For by grace you have been saved through faith, and this is not from you;
> it is the gift of God. (Ephesians 2:8)

Often our misunderstanding stems from the idea that faith is a *gift*, and we perpetuate that *have-havenot* or *light-switch* attitude. We mistakenly think that *some have this gift; others do not.*

Yes, faith is a gift: God invites us to know, love, and serve him. The gift is the *invitation*. Practicing the virtue of faith is our response.

> Faith is the realization of what is hoped for and evidence of things not
> seen. (Hebrews 11:1)

The virtue of faith is concerned with strengthening three areas:
1) Belief – the intellectual understanding of and assent to what we believe
2) Spirituality – the emotional trust in and relationship with God
3) Discipleship – living one's faith out in life, following through with moral actions and a commitment to justice

Sometimes these three dimensions are referred to as the head (belief), heart (spirituality), and hands (discipleship). [Image 2]

Head    Heart    Hands

A person can be stronger or weaker in any one of the three areas. Developing the virtue of faith means that we are called to work on strengthening each of these three areas in our lives.

~~~~~

*Becca had always thought about faith in terms of belief. At 16, she was at a point in her life where she didn't know what she believed, so she felt like she had no faith. Becca's friends would describe her as honest, hard-working, and full of integrity... kind, caring, and committed to social justice. Her behavior aligned with God's will even if she struggled with her intellectual belief. She had never considered her actions to be a way to express and experience faith. Thinking about the virtue in this way allowed her to see that she did, in fact, have faith. It was a starting point. This realization opened her to the possibility of growth in other areas, and ultimately led to healing her relationship with God.*

~~~~~

3. Consider your own practice of the virtue of faith. For each of the three dimensions of faith, where on the continuum of stronger–weaker would you place yourself? Be sure to identify your strengths so that you can see how you are already practicing the virtue of faith.

4. What is one thing you could do to work on strengthening each area of faith?

# Chapter 6

# From Death to New Life

⚜

Catholics use a lot of words and phrases that we don't always stop to unpack and explain. One of these is "the Paschal Mystery." I'm pretty sure that as a child I resigned myself to not understanding what it meant because as it says, it's a mystery.

The Paschal Mystery refers to Jesus' Passion (suffering), Death, Resurrection, and Ascension (into heaven). The very essence of Christian faith revolves around the fact that the suffering and death of Jesus was not the end of the story. Rather, from his death, comes new life in the Resurrection.

Unless a grain of wheat falls to the ground and dies, it remains just a grain of wheat but if it dies, it produces much fruit. (John 12:24)

Death is not the end. It is a mystery because we do not understand how it happens. But it does. And in this mystery we find our salvation: from death to new life.

Moreover, it's not just something that happened to Jesus. God's transforming power in the Paschal Mystery happens in our lives every day. We experience our own cycles of from-death-to-new-life whenever we recover from brokenness.

Sometimes the "death" we experience is literally a loss of a loved one. Other times it's an ending of a friendship, the loss of a job, or a relocation that moves us away from a beloved community. The "ending" might involve a breakup of a special relationship or a divorce. Sometimes it's the end of a hope or dream. Other times it is the conclusion of a chapter in life.

That suffering and death—that pain—is real. Recall the *Agony in the Garden*. As Jesus prayed in the Garden of Gethsemane, he told his disciples, "The sorrow in my heart is so great that it almost crushes me" (Matthew 26:37).[7] How often have we felt that pain?

---

[7] This reference from Matthew 26:37 (and Mark 14:34) comes from the Good News Translation (formerly called the Good News Bible or Today's English Version). This translation was first published in 1976 by the American Bible Society as a "common language" Bible. At Mass on Sunday, we read from the New American Bible Revised Edition (NABRE). In that translation, this same line from Scripture reads, "My soul is sorrowful even to death."

But the suffering and death of Good Friday was not the end. Death did not win. No. Through the transforming power of God, the joy of Easter Sunday brings us new life in the Resurrection. No one was more surprised by this joy than the apostles. They never expected it!

How often have we experienced unforeseen joy in the wake of brokenness?

~~~~~

*DJ had been dating his girlfriend for six years when they broke up. Although their fights had become frequent, he always thought that they would reconcile. In the aftermath of the breakup, DJ became depressed. He couldn't get over the devastation. When he called his sister, he wasn't looking for advice so much as someone to listen.*

*She compassionately recalled her own experience. "When I was in that place, I know it was hard for me want to do anything, so I would watch a lot of mindless TV – whatever movies were on Lifetime or TBS – and it just made me feel worse about myself...like even more of a loser."*

*DJ muttered, "Replace Lifetime with Judge Judy, but yeah, that's where I am."*

*She continued, "It definitely took a while to get through it, but two things that really helped were having a really good counselor to talk to and filling all that 'extra' time that I would've spent with my ex doing something productive, like volunteering. Soon, I became so busy that I didn't have the time to wallow, and it helped me to feel good about what I was doing—even if I didn't feel good about myself. It's not a forever solution, but it was a really helpful next step for me."*

*DJ had seen a sign advertising the need for volunteer firefighters. He had been hesitant, but the conversation with his sister gave him the push he needed; after all, he felt like he had nothing left to lose. After his application was accepted and he began training, he discovered that not only was he good at it, but he loved being a firefighter. Soon, DJ was encouraged by the captain to go to the Fire Academy, and over the next few years he went from a volunteer to a paid, professional firefighter and EMT. From brokenness and despair to hope, passion, and purpose.*

~~~~~

We each have our own story of death-to-new-life. Each time we see that transformation in our own lives, we become aware of how the Paschal Mystery is alive in each of us.

1.  What are some of your own experiences of death-to-new-life? How is the Paschal Mystery alive in you?

Notice that this cycle of death-to-new-life is not something that happens to us once. It is part of our daily lives. We certainly have our big, momentous stories of pain, suffering, and the transforming power of God in our lives. But at any given moment, in every aspect of our daily life, we can find ourselves identifying with some part of the Paschal Mystery. In fact, you many even notice that different areas of your life are in different stages of the death-to-new-life cycle.

When Fr. Ronald Rolheiser, OMI discusses Paschal Mystery Spirituality in *The Holy Longing*, he offers an additional insight about the process of letting go. He refers to the 40 Days between the Resurrection on Easter Sunday and Jesus' Ascension into heaven as a time of transition. New life has begun, but we still need to let go of the old life. Letting go is the Ascension into heaven – no longer clinging on to the past, but really giving it up to God. And finally, at Pentecost, the Holy Spirit comes upon us and we fully embrace the new life.[8]

- The suffering and death in the Passion on Good Friday
- The reception of new life in the Resurrection of Easter Sunday
- Transitioning from grieving the old to adjusting to the new in the Forty Days
- Letting go of the old in the Ascension
- Living out the new life in Pentecost

Sometimes we struggle with the cycle itself. We can get stuck in Good Friday. Or perhaps we are stuck in the 40 Days, never managing to let go of the painful past and experience the Ascension. Some are no longer suffering in the Passion of Good Friday, but they are not yet experiencing new life in the Resurrection... rather, they are in-between, waiting... akin to Holy Saturday.

If you are stuck—or you know someone who is—consider looking into a screening for depression. Parish priests, deacons, and pastoral staff members can help you tend to the spiritual side of getting stuck, and they can also recommend counselors to assist with the very real challenges that depression brings.

A Paschal Mystery spirituality recognizes God's presence throughout this death-to-new-life cycle. When we are in Good Friday, a Paschal Mystery spirituality allows us to call out in the words of Psalm 22:2 – the words Jesus himself prayed on the cross – "My

---

[8] For more on this topic, read Chapter 7 of *The Holy Longing: The Search for a Christian Spirituality* (The Doubleday Religious Publishing Group), by Fr. Ronald Rolheiser, OMI, in which he explains Paschal Mystery Spirituality as a cycle:
    1. Good Friday ... "the loss of life— real death"
    2. Easter Sunday ... "the reception of new life"
    3. The Forty Days ... "a time for readjustment to the new and for grieving the old"
    4. Ascension ... "letting go of the old and letting it bless you, the refusal to cling"
    5. Pentecost ... "the reception of new spirit for the new life that one is already living."

God, my God, why have you abandoned me?" With a Paschal Mystery spirituality, we have hope for new life in the Resurrection. We find encouragement by knowing the Jesus gave the disciples time to grieve and adjust before the Ascension. A Paschal Mystery spirituality trusts that the Holy Spirit will work through us when we come to Pentecost.

2.  Where in the Paschal Mystery are you now? Are the different areas of your life at different moments in the cycle? Explain.

3.  Do you struggle with getting stuck in any part of the Paschal Mystery cycle?

4.  How can you practice a Paschal Mystery spirituality in your own life? What steps will you take?

# Chapter 7

# It's About Relationship, Not Rules

One evening at dinner, I told my boys I was looking forward to giving a lecture at Church on morality. My 6 year old asked: "Mommy, what is mo-wal-ity?"

Though I was prepared to launch into my explanation that *most of us presume morality is about following a set of rules, and it's not... it's about relationship*, in that moment I was challenged to accurately and succinctly describe morality in a way that my 6 and 7 ½ year old boys would understand. "Morality is about what's right and wrong, and why."

Without missing a beat, he tells me: "Oh, Mommy! But you teach me and my brudder about that evewy day!"

I want my kids to be good people, so yes, every day I am concerned with the decisions they make and developing their character–whether they're playing with friends, following through on responsibilities around the house, working at school, or paying attention to the needs of the world around them. Morality is concerned with what's right and wrong, and why, but it's not about rules; it's about relationship.

## Relationship

The reason **WHY** something is right or wrong has everything to do with relationship.

1.  Think about three of your closest friends. What are some of the "unspoken rules" that close friends follow to maintain a healthy relationship? Make a list of these relationship-guiding rules.

As we explore the idea that *relationships* are the reason **WHY** something is considered right or wrong, it makes sense to consider **WHO** is involved and the **HOW**.

**WHO:** Relationship with whom? From the perspective of Christian Morality, we are talking about living a good life in relationship with God. What makes something moral or immoral is *whether it strengthens or damages our relationship with God.* When we say something is a "sin" it's because it damages our relationship with God, *not* because it is "breaking the rules."

**HOW:** So how do we strengthen our relationship with God? By loving, honoring, and respecting God and all of God's Creation. The number one overarching principle that guides our approach to being in *right relationship* is a respect for the value, worth, and special dignity within each person as a child of God, created in the image and likeness of God. Catholic Social Teaching refers to this as ***respect for human dignity***, which finds its Scriptural roots in Genesis.

> God created humankind in his image; in the image of God he created them; male and female he created them. (Genesis 1:27)

As Christians, we are called to respect human dignity with the care and concern of unconditional love.

> This is my commandment: love one another as I love you. (John 15:12)

When we put together the WHO and the HOW of morality, we can see that *living a good life in relationship with God* has three dimensions:

1) **Interpersonal**- respecting the human dignity of others, which is demonstrated by *how we treat one another.*
2) **Personal** – respecting one's own human dignity, which is demonstrated by *how we develop our internal quality of character*
3) **Transcendent** – respecting God, which is demonstrated by *practicing the virtue of faith.*

The Commandments, Beatitudes, and Virtues help flesh out the **WHAT** of Catholic moral teaching with more specifics, but if we don't begin with that understanding of being in right relationship with oneself, others, and the God who created us and loves us, then our approach to morality *will* be limited to simply "following the rules."

2. What attitudes or assumptions do you bring to a discussion of morality? Are they helpful or limiting?

3. Think about your relationship with yourself, with others, and with God. In what ways do you see *love* and *respect for human dignity* guiding your behavior in those relationships? Where do you succeed in practicing this "respect"? Where do you struggle? Is there one area that you feel called to work on improving?

# Chapter 8

# Like vs. Love

✦

*I grew up in a house where we said "I love you" a lot. It was a statement of appreciation ("Thanks, Mom! Love you!"), a farewell ("Love you! Bye"), a part of the bedtime routine from childhood through adulthood, ("Goodnight! I love you!"), as well as an expression of sentiment ("Happy Birthday! I love you!").*

~~~~~

*I frequently tell my husband, kids, siblings, parents, and friends "I love you!" And I mean it sincerely. There is a bright shade of lime-green which I love. I love red wine and dark chocolate. I love bacon. I love my Vita-Mix, my iPhone, and the way my washer and dryer beep me a song when they're finished a cycle (instead of buzzing). I love the city of Austin.*

~~~~~

*One of my close friends recently died of breast cancer. Shortly after we heard of her diagnosis—before she even started chemo—all of the women that she called her "Village" of support gathered together to make a quilt that held messages of love on each square (so that she could wrap herself in our love whenever she needed it). As she waded through treatments and countless appointments, we made meals, helped with childcare, raised funds, prayed, and opened our hearts to do whatever we could…even with the funeral…even after the funeral with her husband and three beautiful children.*

~~~~~

*I remember one time when my son was 3 ½, he got sick in the middle of the night. He came to my bedside and in the saddest, most heartbreaking voice said, "Mommy, I had an accident and it got all over." Without hesitation I jumped up and consoled him. Within a split second of surveying the scene, I called my husband in to care for our son while I cleaned up the mess. The whole thing was quite unpleasant, but handled with tremendous love.*

~~~~~

## What is Love?

With all the different ways we use the word "love," it's a good idea to take a moment to reflect upon what exactly we mean. I am the first to admit my laziness when it comes to distinguishing between like and love. My love of places and things is really about enjoyment, and sometimes that enjoyment is pretty intense.

In English, we have one all-inclusive word for love. In Greek, there are four distinct words. I appreciate the insight that C.S. Lewis gives in *The Four Loves* as he defines and describes each one and their relation to one another.

1) *Storge* – [pronounced with two syllables, and a hard "g" ~ STORE-GAY] A love rooted in a natural fondness or affection which is due in large part because of familiarity. This is often the love we find within families, between parents and children, siblings, or cousins – people who we are with by chance. The expression "blood is thicker than water" reflects *storge* love.

2) *Philia* – [the root word in Philadelphia; pronounced PHILLY-AH] true friendship love, involving loyalty, equality, respect, and the bonds of shared interests and activities.

3) *Eros* – [the root word of erotic ~ ERR-OS] refers to a passionate love. This is certainly the intimate love of romance, but it is not necessarily sexual. Eros refers to the passionate love which touches the depths of one's soul with excitement, energy, and beauty.

4) *Agape* [pronounced as AH-GAP-AY or AH-GAH-PAY] is the unconditional giving of oneself—selflessly—for the good of another.

As we come to understand the different kinds of love, we shouldn't feel the need to categorize a relationship or even a given experience as exclusively one of the four kinds of love. There is often quite a bit of overlap.

~~~~~

*I find myself quite fortunate to have all four kinds of love for my husband. When we dated, our friendship grew as we discovered our mutual appreciation of live music and outdoor fun. The mutual respect that followed offered us a great foundation for philia, which we continually cultivate with quality time. Over time, we developed eros, with a passionate and energetic connection that feeds my spirit. I joke that "fondness" for his geeky ways as an aerospace engineer is why I have storge for him—that and I've gotten used to him always being around, but in truth, the loyalty and affection I have for him is rooted in commitment. And we undoubtedly practice agape with each other, with our children, and with the world around us.*

~~~~~

All love is good; we needn't rate the four loves as superior and inferior. What we should do, however, is pay attention to the differences. Why? Just as we can get ourselves into trouble when we confuse *love* with *like*, things can also go awry when we confuse *philia* with *agape* (thinking we have to be friends with everybody).

In faith, we are called to "Love one another as I have loved you" (John 13:34). But Jesus was not calling us to practice *eros, storge,* or *philia.* Jesus loves us with *agape* and calls us to practice *agape*—unconditional care and concern for the well-being of another—with those we encounter.[9] *Agape* is the theological virtue of which St. Paul speaks in his First Letter to the Corinthians. Recognizing it as a virtue means that *agape* is the kind of love we can choose to practice, and become better at practicing.

1. *Who* do you love? Make a quick list of five people. As you think about *who* you love, consider also *how* you love. Indicate which loves you practice with each person.

2. Describe a time when you practiced agape towards someone you were not friends with. How does reflecting on that experience help you see how to practice agape for someone you struggle with?

---

[9] Recall the post-Resurrection "Do you love me?" exchange between Peter and Jesus (John 21:15-19). We know that this threefold exchange counteracts Peter's threefold denial after Jesus' arrest. Interestingly, there is a distinction in the Greek word for love that is used which gives us an additional insight. The first two times Jesus asked Peter, "Do you *agape* me?" and Peter replied, "Yes, Lord, you know that I *philia* you." The third time Jesus changes his word: "Do you *philia* me?" and Peter replied with the same, "I *philia* you." Jesus asks us to *agape* love, but will meet us where we are and accept whatever kind of love we are capable of giving.

3.  Which of the four loves do you find abundantly in your life? Which do you find yourself being nudged to cultivate more of and why?

4.  Choose a situation (at home, at work, with friends, in your commute, etc.) that would benefit from more of your agape love. What will you do to make that happen?

# Chapter 9

# Called By God

Before I formed you in the womb I knew you, before you were born I dedicated you. (Jeremiah 1:5)

God created you. You are a child of God, created in God's image and likeness. You have inherent value and worth as a child of God. Fr. Richard Rohr, OFM explains the depth of what human dignity means:

> You are a son or daughter of the Good and Loving God. The Divine Image is planted inherently and intrinsically within you. You cannot create it, you cannot manufacture it, you cannot earn it, you cannot achieve it, you cannot attain it, you cannot cumulatively work up to it. Do you know why? Because you already have it! That is the core of the Gospel.[10]

1. Previous chapters have touched upon the importance of respecting human dignity. How well do you practice respecting *your own* human dignity?

To respect your own human dignity means to have a healthy self-love: recognizing your own gifts, talents, and goodness as a creation of God. Healthy self-love is far from boastfulness or arrogant self-pride. Rather, it is recognizing and believing in the truth and goodness of God's creation.

---

[10] From Richard Rohr's Daily Meditation on April 14, 2014, "Transformative Dying: Collapsing into the Larger Life," available through his Center for Action and Contemplation (cac.org). Adapted from *Dying: We Need It for Life*. http://myemail.constantcontact.com/Richard-Rohr-s-Meditation--Collapsing-into-the-Larger-Life.html?soid=1103098668616&aid=SZvXjpOEWkU Accessed April 23, 2014.

For some of us, self-love is hard. Perhaps it's because of how we were treated by our family in our formative years… Perhaps it is because of childhood trauma… Perhaps it's because we believe the lies of inadequacy that the media tells us with unabashed consistency (so that we will be sure to buy whatever products we need to make ourselves look and feel better…)

Then God asked: Who told you that you were naked? (Genesis 3:11)

For whatever reason we may struggle with self-love and respecting our own human dignity, it is important that we understand that sense of shame, inadequacy, and self-hatred is not from God.

Moreover, it is important that we work on healing this spiritual weakness, as a matter of faith. While our understanding of morality and the call to social justice extend from respecting the human dignity in others, our understanding of *vocation* and *calling* extend from respecting our human dignity within.

Vocation refers to the sense of being called by God to do something. What are we called to? In faith, we understand that all of us—all of humankind—are called to holiness, which simply means to be set aside and dedicated to God. Holiness is not about being flawless or perfect, but rather being dedicated to seeking God. Chapter 3 noted that this *seeking* is more about the process of conversion than spiritual perfectionism.

We are called to live our lives as either married, single, or religious. In Church, we often pray for *an increase in vocations to the priesthood*, but what many don't realize is that we are praying for each person to listen to the call of God within. God is calling *you* to live as either a married person, a single person, or in religious life (as a priest, brother, sister, monk or nun). One of those ways of life is how you will best be able to live out your call to holiness. Each one is a calling.

> There are different kinds of spiritual gifts but the same Spirit; there are different forms of service but the same Lord; there are different workings but the same God who produces all of them in everyone. To each individual the manifestation of the Spirit is given for some benefit. (1 Corinthians 12:4-7)

In addition to being called to a way of life, you are called to use your unique set of gifts and talents. This sense of vocational calling often leads us to a certain career path or profession, but vocation is not the same thing as a job. While some may feel called to a career in education or medicine, others live out their vocation serving God as a stay-at-home-mom or through volunteering. Sometimes we are able to make a living by doing what we are passionate about; other times we might work a job for financial security and spend our "free" time doing the thing that makes our heart happy.

~~~~~

*Mary was a dance major in college; she loved to dance and was good at it. But it wasn't until she began teaching dance that she found her passion. It was difficult to make a living as a dance instructor, particularly as she felt called to open her own studio and work more closely with her dancers. However, Mary found that her part-time job working for a pharmacy was giving her the financial security she needed to do what she loved. It was a win-win.*

~~~~~

We are called to know, love, and serve God by using our gifts and talents. In God's infinite wisdom, by God's very design, this happens when we do the thing we are most passionate about.

2. What sense of calling do you have? What gifts and talents do you have? What are you passionate about?

3. Tell of a time when you used your gifts and talents to do what you are passionate about. What does this experience teach you about God? About joy?

We have each been given a unique set of gifts and talents to use in our life—with the people we encounter, in the roles we have. Often we are tempted to doubt or downplay our gifts and talents because we know someone else that is better at *thus-and-such* or because we are aware of our limitations. Hear Jesus emphasize the importance of using the gifts God has given you in the Parable of the Talents:

A man who was going on a journey called in his servants and entrusted his possessions to them. To one he gave five talents; to another, two; to a third, one—to each according to his ability. Then he went away. Immediately the one who received five talents went and traded with them, and made another five. Likewise, the one who received two made another two. But the man who received one went off and dug a hole in the ground and buried his master's money. After a long time the master of those servants came back and settled accounts with them. The one who had received five talents came forward bringing the additional five. He said, "Master, you gave me five talents. See, I have made five more." His master said to him, "Well done, my good and faithful servant. Since you were faithful in small matters, I will give you great responsibilities. Come, share your master's joy." Then the one who had received two talents also came forward and said, "Master, you gave me two talents. See, I have made two more." His master said to him, "Well done, my good and faithful servant. Since you were faithful in small matters, I will give you great responsibilities. Come, share your master's joy." Then the one who had received the one talent came forward and said, "Master, I knew you were a demanding person, harvesting where you did not plant and gathering where you did not scatter; so out of fear I went off and buried your talent in the ground. Here it is back." His master said to him in reply, "You wicked, lazy servant! So you knew that I harvest where I did not plant and gather where I did not scatter? Should you not then have put my money in the bank so that I could have got it back with interest on my return? Now then! Take the talent from him and give it to the one with ten. For to everyone who has, more will be given and he will grow rich; but from the one who has not, even what he has will be taken away. And throw this useless servant into the darkness outside, where there will be wailing and grinding of teeth." (Matthew 25:14-30)

We are expected to do our best with what we have been given in the circumstances which we find ourselves. We are not all given the same gifts. Nor are we all expected to bear the same "fruits" with our labor. Rather, we are to do our best with what we have been given.

When you are tempted to allow your awareness of your imperfections and limitations become a stumbling block to following your passion and using your gifts and talents, know that you are in good company. Throughout Scripture, God gives us example after example of how he works in, with, and through our imperfections, such as Moses, the prophets, the disciples, and St. Paul, just to name a few.

4.  When it comes to gifts, talents, and passion, what stumbling blocks do you struggle with?

5.  What insight do you take from this reflection for your own life? Is there something that you feel "called" to do? What steps will you take?

# Chapter 10

# Prayer as Conversation

⚜

Prayer is how we communicate with God. It is sacred conversation: God initiates a dialogue with us and prayer is our response. The traditional definition of prayer is "the raising of one's mind and heart to God" (CCC, 2559). Prayer is the essence of "a vital and personal relationship with the living and true God" (CCC 2558).

> "For me, prayer is a surge of the heart; it is a simple look turned toward heaven, it is a cry of recognition and of love, embracing both trial and joy."
> —St. Thérèse of Lisieux

1.  What is prayer for you? How would you describe what prayer is?

2.  Where did you get your understanding of prayer from? In what ways does your understanding of prayer help (or hinder) your relationship with God?

Catholic tradition identifies four different kinds of prayer: petition, praise, contrition, and thanksgiving. We are probably most familiar with petition, in which we are asking God for what we need. Prayers of thanksgiving usually follow when we actually get what we are asking for. However, this sort of prayer goes much deeper than that. The

Mass is the ultimate prayer of thanksgiving, in which we offer gratitude for all that God has given us: life, faith, redemption, for one another, for this earth. Prayers of praise, or adoration, truly recognize God's majesty; we often do this more in a meditative or contemplative way of being than through words alone. In prayers of contrition, we acknowledge our failures and express our sorrow for our sins.

> 3. Think about your own practice of prayer. What kinds of prayer do you most frequently employ?

Communication involves both talking and listening. Sometimes our prayer life can be a little talk-heavy and lacking in listening. Catholic Tradition not only offers a wealth of formulaic prayers and devotions, we also have an abundance of resources to assist with meditation and contemplation.

With meditation, we focus on something, such as a passage from Scripture or the words of a saint or holy person. With contemplation, we open our hearts and minds to receive God. Most of us have a hard time turning down the noise in our brains, so the practice of meditation helps bring us to a place where we can actually open ourselves to contemplation.

*Lectio Divina*, Latin for "divine reading" or "holy reading" [pronounced LEX-EE-OH DI-VEE-NAH], is an ancient Catholic practice of reading and praying with Scripture which can be done in groups or individually. To practice *lectio divina*, begin by selecting a passage from Scripture; many use the one of the readings of the day, others decide to slowly work through a book of the Bible. Feel free to choose any passage. Settle into a quiet space and like rungs of a ladder, work through these four stages, reading and re-reading the passage, amid interludes of silence.

1) *lectio* – READ the passage slowly and reflectively (several times) so that it sinks in.
2) *meditatio* – REFLECT on a word or phrase from the passage, meditating on it, memorizing it, repeating it to yourself.
3) *oratio* – RESPOND by allowing the meditation to lead you into a prayerful conversation with God, letting go of thoughts and opening your heart to listening.

4) *contemplatio* – REST in the presence of God… the Word of God… the embrace of God… be in the openness of contemplation.[11]

For instance, if you were to choose Psalm 46:10 "Be still and know that I am God," you might first read and repeat that line several times. As you reflect, you might shorten the Psalm until one word or phrase stands out: "be still and know that I am…" "Be still and know…" "Be still…" "Be." Meditating on that word brings you to a place of response, and finally rest.

Prayer can happen anywhere, anytime. Another prayerful practice is to reflect upon your day, inviting God to speak to you through your reflection. Whether this happens at Church in adoration, in your favorite chair in your living room, in your commute, or in the shower, prayer happens when we communicate with God.

In addition to asking God's blessing on meals, my husband and I have started practicing a prayerful dinner-time conversation with our young boys that incorporates this kind of reflection, called "The Rose," which is a loose adaptation of St. Ignatius Loyola's Examen.[12] At the dinner table, one person leads by being the first to share their "rose," and then invites everyone else to follow suit. The reflection continues with each person's "bud," "thorn," and "root."

- Rose – the parts of your day that you are thankful for
- Bud – something you are looking forward to in the coming days or weeks
- Thorn – a difficult part of your day (*that you might ask God's help with*)
- Root – something you are hoping and praying for

We conclude our dinner-time conversation by saying, "*Thank you for our rose, bless our bud, hear our root, and help us with our thorn.*" I appreciate how the rose offers children and adults a structure for sharing their day—with one another and with God—as it gently fosters reflection and gratitude.

---

[11] For more information on *lectio divina*, visit the Order of Carmelites website http://ocarm.org/en/content/lectio/what-lectio-divina (Accessed May 27, 2014).

[12] Heidi Clark and Sara Fontana at St. Paul the Apostle Catholic Church in Houston, Texas are credited with teaching me "The Rose." The Ignatian Spirituality website provides an overview of the Examen. "The Daily Examen is a technique of prayerful reflection on the events of the day in order to detect God's presence and discern his direction for us. The Examen is an ancient practice in the Church that can help us see God's hand at work in our whole experience. The method presented [below] is adapted from a technique described by Ignatius Loyola in his Spiritual Exercises.
1. Become aware of God's presence.
2. Review the day with gratitude.
3. Pay attention to your emotions.
4. Choose one feature of the day and pray from it.
5. Look toward tomorrow."
Accessed May 28, 2014 http://www.ignatianspirituality.com/ignatian-prayer/the-examen/.

4.   What prayerful practice(s) have you found most helpful?  Why?

5.   What prayerful practice did you read or learn about that you would like to try?

# Chapter 11

# Spiritual Crisis

We all go through difficult times. Pain and brokenness make their way into everyone's story.

When the pain and suffering lead to a conversion experience and new life in Christ, we almost find it easier to reconcile the idea of the suffering… but when we go through a darkness *after* or *despite* doing our best to live a life of faith, it can be troubling.

~~~~~

*My lowest-low time came when I was 24 years old. Just three weeks short of what would have been my first wedding anniversary, my spouse never came home one evening, which in itself was significant, but it was a pressing concern because we had plans to drive to his sister's for an overnight visit. Upon returning close to midnight, he casually responded to an offhand remark I made by revealing that he didn't want to be married, had never wanted to get married, and thought we should just "break-up." I was not only committed to my Catholic faith, but I had specific, poignant conversations with this man during our 17 month engagement about the Sacrament of Marriage, about the Covenant which we would be entering into, and about how divorce was not an option. Not for me, anyhow. I thought I was on the right path. I thought I was doing the right thing. How could God have allowed this to happen to me?*

~~~~~

While everyone experiences pain and suffering, not everyone necessarily goes through a spiritual crisis. However, for those that have—or for those who currently find themselves in the midst of one—it can be unsettling.

1. Have you ever gone through a spiritual crisis? What was going on? Why would you describe it as a spiritual crisis?

If you *have* ever gone through what Christian tradition calls a spiritual darkness, or "the dark night of the soul," fear not; you are in good company.

- **St. John of the Cross** is credited with the expression "dark night of the soul." In 1577, John was abducted, imprisoned, and tortured for his part in working on reforms to the Carmelite Order. While in prison, John composed the poem *Dark Night of the Soul.*

- **St. Teresa of Ávila** was a close friend and contemporary of St. John of the Cross. After unexpectedly healing from a serious illness and professing great devotion to St. Joseph, Teresa began struggling so deeply with spiritual darkness that she stopped praying for nearly two years.

- **C.S. Lewis** wrote about his spiritual darkness in *A Grief Observed.* After years as an author, theologian, and expert in Christian apologetics, Lewis married his longtime friend Joy, who died of cancer only four years after they wed.

- **Mother Teresa** experienced a spiritual darkness that lasted for decades, which began shortly after she founded the Missionaries of Charity and started her work with the poor.[13]

"If I ever become a Saint—I will surely be one of 'darkness.' I will continually be absent from Heaven—to light the light of those in darkness on earth." —Mother Teresa of Calcutta

2. Do you find the idea that saints and holy people have struggled with the dark night of the soul encouraging or troubling? Why?

Shortly after composing his poem, St. John of the Cross escaped imprisonment and went on to write a Treatise on *The Dark Night of the Soul,* offering theological commentary stanza-by-stanza. St. John's insights on the experience of the dark night are worth noting.

---

[13] Mother Teresa's book *Come Be My Light: The Private Writings of the "Saint of Calcutta"* (Doubleday, 2007) details her interior life through her personal journals. Published after her death in 2005, it is edited by Brian Kolodiejchuk.

The dark night is not a punishment, nor does it refer to a sinful, sinister darkness. Rather, as saints and holy people alike have experienced it, it is part of a process—part of the journey to God.

One of the characteristics of this darkness is the feeling of spiritual emptiness because whatever you used to do to feel connected with God no longer works.

> Prayer that used to be full of consolation and peace may now seem empty and dry. Worship and other church activities are not as rewarding as they used to be. It is increasingly difficult to maintain daily "active" practices like prayer, meditation, journaling, or spiritual reading. In general, one finds oneself losing interest in the spiritual things that used to offer so much gratification. Even the images of God one has depended upon may gradually lose their significance.[14]

The darkness is compounded by the feeling that we must be doing something wrong; we are plagued by self-doubt. It should come as no surprise that depression often accompanies spiritual darkness.

St. John encourages us to see that the dark night of the soul is an opportunity to do some spiritual spring cleaning. So whatever *way you had thought about God* is not working? Let that thought go. Empty yourself of all that you cling to. Liberate yourself from attachment to rigidly held beliefs, expectations, or dreams.

~~~~~

*Jean has struggled with the pain of infertility: "Growing up there was no doubt in my mind that all I wanted to be was a wife and mother, and I fully expected that to be my life as an adult. I loved children and they loved me. I was going to be the perfect parent. As I got older and my 'good husband prospects' didn't seem to be appearing, I even started to think about becoming a single mother. After kissing way too many 'toads,' I finally found my prince charming. Despite the fleeting child-bearing years, I still fully believed we would have a family together and didn't start to panic until a solid year of fertility drugs, procedures, and even a failed in-vitro. The option to adopt was not a viable one for us. I had to face facts – I was never going to be a mother. The pain of this reality and the hole it has left in my heart will never go away, but I have been able to move on. I used to tearfully rant about God not being fair, but I just don't think this was God. Believing in a God who is cruel and evil was even worse than not being able to have babies. With that mentality I would never have a soft place to land. It just didn't work, and I would need to find another outlet for my 'motherly' instincts. And I needed to not be angry with God, but to be happy about all the other wonderful*

---

[14] Gerald G. May, *The Dark Night of the Soul: A Psychiatrist Explores the Connection Between Darkness and Spiritual Growth* (HarperCollins Publishers, 2004), page 88. In his book, May describes Teresa and John's background, journeys, experiences, and insights with the dark night of the soul.

*things in my life. We are quick to blame God but not as quick to appreciate and thank Him for our blessings."*

~ ~ ~ ~ ~

A spiritual darkness can help us understand that we are not in control, especially not when it comes to God's grace. Recall the Parable of the Workers in the Vineyard.

> The kingdom of heaven is like a landowner who went out at dawn to hire laborers for his vineyard. After agreeing with them for the usual daily wage, he sent them into his vineyard. Going out about nine o'clock, he saw others standing idle in the marketplace, and he said to them, "You too go into my vineyard, and I will give you what is just." So they went off. [And] he went out again around noon, and around three o'clock, and did likewise. Going out about five o'clock, he found others standing around, and said to them, "Why do you stand here idle all day?" They answered, "Because no one has hired us." He said to them, "You too go into my vineyard." When it was evening the owner of the vineyard said to his foreman, "Summon the laborers and give them their pay, beginning with the last and ending with the first." When those who had started about five o'clock came, each received the usual daily wage. So when the first came, they thought that they would receive more, but each of them also got the usual wage. And on receiving it they grumbled against the landowner, saying, "These last ones worked only one hour, and you have made them equal to us, who bore the day's burden and the heat." He said to one of them in reply, "My friend, I am not cheating you. Did you not agree with me for the usual daily wage? Take what is yours and go. What if I wish to give this last one the same as you? [Or] am I not free to do as I wish with my own money? Are you envious because I am generous?" Thus, the last will be first, and the first will be last. (Matthew 20:1-16)

The workers think they "deserve" something more because of their efforts, but that's not how God works. We don't earn it. God's Kingdom is offered to us, and we either say yes or no. God loves, gives, and forgives with generosity. That is the gift of God's grace. If you find yourself struggling with this, ask yourself: *Am I envious because God is generous?*

3. When it comes to spiritual spring cleaning, what do you need to let go of?

# Chapter 12

# Love and Judgment of Others

⅄

You know the Parable of the Good Samaritan?  We hear the parable calling us to help others in need, but in the set-up and delivery of the parable, Jesus is telling us a whole lot more.

First, the set-up: There was a scholar of the law that was testing Jesus, asking what he needs to do to inherit eternal life.  Jesus knows that this guy knows the answer, so like any good teacher, he answers with a question, and the scholar replies with what we call "The Greatest Commandment."

> There was a scholar of the law who stood up to test him and said, "Teacher, what must I do to inherit eternal life?"  Jesus said to him, "What is written in the law? How do you read it?" He said in reply, "You shall love the Lord, your God, with all your heart, with all your being, with all your strength, and with all your mind, and your neighbor as yourself."  He replied to him, "You have answered correctly; do this and you will live." (Luke 10:25-28)

When Jesus responds with the parable, he makes the hero out to be the person everyone loves to hate: the Samaritan.  And he paints the ones everyone would assume to be the hero as negligent.

> But because he wished to justify himself, he said to Jesus, "And who is my neighbor?" Jesus replied, "A man fell victim to robbers as he went down from Jerusalem to Jericho. They stripped and beat him and went off leaving him half-dead.  A priest happened to be going down that road, but when he saw him, he passed by on the opposite side.  Likewise a Levite came to the place, and when he saw him, he passed by on the opposite side.  But a Samaritan traveler who came upon him was moved with compassion at the sight.  He approached the victim, poured oil and wine over his wounds and bandaged them. Then he lifted him up on his own animal, took him to an inn and cared for him.  The next day he took out two silver coins and gave them to the innkeeper with the instruction, 'Take

care of him. If you spend more than what I have given you, I shall repay you on my way back.' Which of these three, in your opinion, was neighbor to the robbers' victim?" He answered, "The one who treated him with mercy." Jesus said to him, "Go and do likewise." (Luke 10:29-37)

Why the hatred of Samaritans? Think of two groups of people that simply don't get along for reasons that are long and complicated. Here, the reasons were rooted in both religion and politics, dating more than 900 years before the time of Jesus. It takes a bit of understanding the historical, cultural context of the day to fully comprehend how *justified* the Jews felt in their hatred of the Samaritans – to the point of considering them traitors and calling them "dogs" and "half-breeds."

In this parable, Jesus is not only calling upon us to help those in need, but he is also telling us to let go of prejudice and hate.[15] Letting go of prejudice and hate can be difficult, especially if you were raised in an environment where that was the norm. Yet, that is exactly what we are called to do.

1. When it comes to the topic of prejudice, what was the example(s) that you were given? What have you chosen to imitate? What have you chosen to change? Why?

Prejudices are rooted in stereotypes. A stereotype is a generalization about a person or group of people based on incomplete knowledge. Our brains naturally like to categorize people, places, and things into groups so that we are able to quickly make sense of the world around us. As general categories, stereotypes can be positive (*Asians are good at math*) or negative (*white men can't jump*).

The problem comes in when we forget (or ignore) the fact that we *are* making assumptions, and the information *is* incomplete, such that we treat our stereotypes as truth.

---

[15] Jesus also challenges his disciples to let go of prejudice in his encounter with the Samaritan woman in John 4:9. The website Catholic Answers details many more examples in the New Testament about the tension between the two groups as well as Jesus' insistence on a new attitude towards Samaritans. See http://www.catholic.com/quickquestions/who-were-the-samaritans-and-why-were-they-important. (Accessed May 31, 2014). For more about the 900+ year rift, including Old Testament citations, visit St. Anthony Messenger's website http://www.americancatholic.org/messenger/sep1996/wiseman.asp. (Accessed May 31, 2014).

Pausing to remind ourselves that we *are* making assumptions can go a long way towards raising our consciousness. Because it is when these unchecked generalizations lead to our *attitudes* towards people and they become prejudices. Far too often, we don't even realize that we have prejudicial attitudes.

Prejudices are attitudes towards people based on stereotypes, such as racism, sexism, ageism, etc. When we treat a stereotype as truth, our prejudicial attitudes require people to prove their unique self-worth to us. As a whole, prejudicial attitudes violate the principle of respect for human dignity.

The Church has specifically declared individual forms of prejudice evil in various letters and documents. For example, the U.S. Catholic Bishops opened their Pastoral Letter *Brothers and Sisters to Us* (1979) by unequivocally stating that racism is evil.

> Racism is a sin: a sin that divides the human family, blots out the image of God among specific members of that family, and violates the fundamental human dignity of those called to be children of the same Father. Racism is the sin that says some human beings are inherently superior and others essentially inferior because of races. It is the sin that makes racial characteristics the determining factor for the exercise of human rights. It mocks the words of Jesus: "Treat others the way you would have them treat you." Indeed, racism is more than a disregard for the words of Jesus; it is a denial of the truth of the dignity of each human being revealed by the mystery of the Incarnation.[16]

Discrimination occurs when we act upon our prejudicial attitudes – giving preferential treatment to one group and excluding another.

> Every form of social or cultural discrimination in fundamental personal rights on the grounds of sex, race, color, social conditions, language, or religion must be curbed and eradicated as incompatible with God's design (CCC, 1935).

2. When it comes to the topic of stereotypes, prejudice, and discrimination, what do you struggle with?

---

[16] *Brothers And Sisters To Us*, the USCCB Pastoral Letter on Racism is available on the USCCB website. http://www.usccb.org/issues-and-action/cultural-diversity/african-american/brothers-and-sisters-to-us.cfm. (Accessed May 31, 2014.)

When we begin to analyze our own behavior with stereotypes, prejudice, and discrimination, there are four basic roles people play:

- **The Target** is on the receiving end of prejudice or bias.
- **The Perpetrator** is the wrong-doer or offender; this is the person who is guilty of telling the racist joke, of being the bully, of being prejudiced towards someone else.
- **The Bystander** witnesses the act, but does not interrupt… stands idly by and stays silent.
- **The Ally** stands up for the target, speaks up and interrupts the act of prejudice or bias.[17]

Our Christian faith calls upon us to not only avoid the sin of being the perpetrator, but to move from the complacency of the bystander to acting with the love and courage of the ally.

3. Think about your own experience with each of these roles. Recall a time when you were:
- The Target

- The Perpetrator

- The Bystander

- The Ally

---

[17] The "Roles People Play" comes from the Anti-Defamation League (ADL), which is an organization dedicated to eradicating prejudice, giving particular focus to the ways in which stereotypes escalate and can lead to violence and genocide. The ADL has partnered with the U.S. Catholic Bishops to help Catholic educators teach about Anti-Semitism, Anti-Judaism, and the Holocaust, particularly in their *Bearing Witness* program. In their anti-bias training, the ADL offers a way to examine the roles people play when it comes to situations involving stereotypes, prejudice, and discrimination. See http://archive.adl.org/education/holocaust/rolespeopleplayworksheet.pdf. (Accessed May 31, 2014).

4.  Which was the most difficult to recall?  Why?

5.  Identify some ways in which you can be an ally in your own life in the coming weeks.

# Chapter 13

# Love in Relationships

When we think of the Christian call to love, we are both inspired by the call and aware of the depth of challenge. *Agape*—the unconditional care and concern for the well-being of others—is beautiful, and when we engage in doing it, we experience the divine. For some reason, however, when we start talking about *love in relationships*, particularly "falling in love," we have a very difficult time making sense of how to integrate the Christian call to love with all of these feelings. We get confused and end up using the models of romantic love that the media offers us as the norm. Whether you are married, single, or religious, a healthier understanding of romantic love is in order. Perhaps it will help to enrich and affirm your relationships... perhaps it will help you process what is happening in your own lived experience, perhaps – if for nothing else – a renewed understanding of romantic love will help you process the misguided media messages.

> 1. In what ways do you agree with the idea that romantic love is confusing? In what ways do you disagree?

Falling in love is simultaneously one of the *most fun* and *most confusing* experiences in life. The butterflies... the smiles... the overwhelming elation... the excitement... It often catches us by surprise—we neither *see it coming* nor *choose* it. It just happens. Sometimes we fall for people that (for whatever reason) we shouldn't. And before we know it, we find ourselves either singing along to *You've Lost That Lovin' Feeling* or being serenaded (and not in the good, fun *Top Gun* way). Add in a few *Three's Company* style misunderstandings or a *Romeo and Juliet* conflict-of-loyalty and you've got the plot to a bulk of the romantic movies, sitcoms, and dramas out there.

No wonder we find it so shocking that *Love is not a feeling*. Even that passionate kind of love known as *eros* discussed in Chapter 8 is not a feeling. This is not to say that love is devoid of feeling. In fact, when we love, it feels *great*. As we understand love, as we teach children about love, as we practice love in our relationships, it would be so much healthier if we understood that feelings *are* a fantastic side effect of loving, but feelings *are not* the essence of love itself.

So how do we live out the call to love and honor our Christian identity in relationships? How does a Christian navigate through the *feelings of falling in love* with integrity?

When it comes to the topic of "Falling in 'Love,'" M. Scott Peck says, "Of all the misconceptions about love the most powerful and pervasive is the belief that 'falling in love' is love…It is a potent misconception."[18] In his bestselling book *The Road Less Traveled*, Peck dedicates a whole section to love. While Peck never used the word *agape*, his explanation certainly aligns with that Greek term for love:

> Love is the will to extend one's self for the purpose of nurturing one's own or another's spiritual growth.[19]

This definition is packed with meaning:

- **Love has a distinct purpose; the goal of love is spiritual growth.** It's not about forcing (yourself or) someone else to fit into your image of what they should be. But about encouraging them to become their very best selves, in God's divine image. Notice the word-choice here: *nurturing…* not implementing, evoking, or creating this change (in oneself or others), but nurturing. That's significant.

- **Love is a circular process: the more we practice extending one's self, the better we become at doing it.** It's easy to think that the circular process refers to "the more you give, the more you get." But that's not what this means. Instead, think of it as extending your limits and expanding your ability to love—akin to working a muscle. The more you work it, the stronger it gets.

- **Real love necessitates self-love.** The ability to truly love necessitates respecting your own human dignity because love is about giving of one's self, and you can't give what you don't have.

---

[18] M. Scott Peck (d. 2005) discussed romantic love in *The Road Less Traveled* (New York: Simon and Schuster, 1978), page 84.
[19] Peck first defines love on page 81, and goes on to explain the five-part definition in the pages that follow.

- **Real love requires effort.** Anytime you "extend your limits" or "expand your ability" to do something, it requires effort. Many people read this with a tinge of negativity, thinking: "effort" means work, and "work" means drudgery. But a lot of wonderfully fun things that we do require effort. What's that cliché? Anything worth doing is worth doing well. Love is something that is worth doing well, and that implies effort.

- **Love is an act of the will; it is a choice.** Love is a decision; it is a choice you make, particularly when we are talking about nurturing one's own or another's spiritual growth.

2. Which parts of Peck's definition resonate with your own experience? What part(s) do you struggle with?

Spending time unpacking M. Scott Peck's definition of love helps us better understand that love is not a feeling, but rather feelings are a pleasant side effect of love.[20] Look at the wording of the expression itself: *falling in love*. A person doesn't "fall" into the kind of *agape* love which Jesus Christ calls us to; that is a choice.

Perhaps it would be better to think of this "falling" as an opportunity for *agape* and *eros*, but not actual love itself. Relationships have a tendency to work their way through a cycle of attraction, differences, disappointments, decisions, and then arrive at the actual experience of love. For the benefit of the visual learners, it might be helpful to offer a diagram what a relationship might look like, and where feelings fit in to the picture.

---

[20] Mistaking the feelings associated with "falling in love" as the essence of real love contradicts every aspect of Peck's definition. Falling in love has no purpose; it "has little to do with…nurturing one's spiritual development" (89). There is no extension of one's self (circular process) with falling in love. Falling in love does not necessitate self-love. Falling in love is effortless – it happens *to* us. Falling in love is not a choice; we don't choose who we do or do not have feelings for.

## The Relationship Cycle [Image 3]

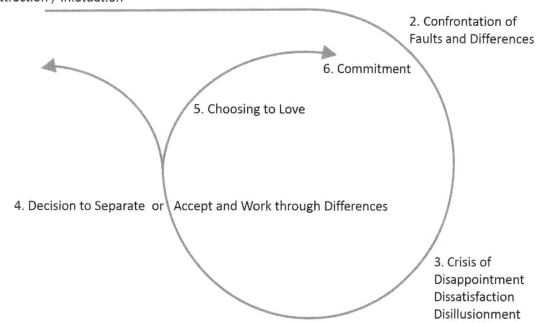

1. Attraction / Infatuation

2. Confrontation of Faults and Differences

6. Commitment

5. Choosing to Love

4. Decision to Separate  or  Accept and Work through Differences

3. Crisis of Disappointment Dissatisfaction Disillusionment

The explanation of the Relationship Cycle reads like the story of an actual relationship:[21]

1) **Attraction/Infatuation** – This is that "beginning of the relationship," where the pair becomes increasingly attracted to one other…also known as "falling in love." As the straight line indicates, this is often the easy phase where everything is wonderfully agreeable. Most of us (subconsciously) are on our best "job-interview" behavior, either overlooking or overcompensating for any possible "faults," because we're in love and everything is perfect!

2) **Confrontation of Faults and Differences** – Whether it's as meaningless as what movie to see or as meaningful as the role of children, money, careers, religion, etc., this is where the couple begins to identify and confront their differences. Many people look at this and exclaim, "Ooooo – first fight!" Perhaps… or perhaps it's just a quiet recognition of the truth… Here, we often hear someone say something to the effect of: "You're not who I thought you were." Somewhere in-between phase one and two, the "falling in love" feeling begins to fade.

3) **Crisis of Disappointment/Dissatisfaction/Disillusionment** – As the ease of the so-called honeymoon ends, it can be disappointing. Devastating, even. This is when we hear the words, "We need to talk."

[21] The "Relationship Cycle" comes from Chapter 5 of Mary McCarty's *Loving: A Catholic Perspective on Vocational Lifestyle Choices* (Brown-Roa, 1993), page 149.

4) **Acceptance or Separation/Abandonment of the Relationship** – At this point, the couple has a choice to work out their differences or decide that the relationship is over. The key here is honesty. Ignoring problems or lying to yourself or your significant other about "working out the differences" doesn't actually bring the relationship to the next phase. That kind of behavior is not only a violation of the Eighth Commandment, but it's just prolonging the inevitable.

5) **Love** – The most obvious implication here is that love is a choice. Love is a verb; it is something you *do*. With the effort of working through differences, the couple truly *chooses* to love one another, the result of which feels wonderful!

6) **Commitment** – The cycle continues… as the couple keeps discovering more and more about one another, they will continue have a choice to make: work it out or abandon the relationship. Commitment is a matter of *continually choosing to love* at every turn.

The Relationship Cycle helps us really see that the "falling in 'love'" phase is just the fun beginning. The real love of *agape* and the passion of *eros* is a lot deeper than that. Real love is a choice which embraces truth and truly feels incredible.

3. Can you relate to the analysis and diagram of the Relationship Cycle? Explain.

4. How does the insight that "love is not a feeling" sit with you? Does it resonate or do you struggle with it?

5.  Where can you look (in your own life or in the media) for examples of real,
    true love?  Can you think of songs, movies or television shows that
    demonstrate true love?  How about examples demonstrating the illusion of
    mistaking the feelings for love?

6.  When it comes to love and relationships, what do you feel called to do?

# Chapter 14

# Sin and Mercy

✦

It was a Theology Q&A session on a retreat – a safe environment. Participants were encouraged to write down their questions on any faith-related topic and submit them anonymously. The group was encouraged to raise hands and ask additional questions if needed. This was their time. There were over 30 retreatants, plus the team; women ranging from their early 20's to their early 80's. When the topic of sin came up, you could feel the emotional intensity in the room. As each question was answered, seven more hands shot up asking questions.

When people ask, "Is it a mortal sin if…" more often than not, they are asking out of fear. Somewhere along the line they learned that ___ was a mortal sin, and if you did [*this thing*], you were going to hell. Some ask the question while thinking about their own behavior; others ask out of concern for a loved one. All ask the question out of fear.

On the one hand, sin is real; we cannot pretend that "anything goes." On the other hand, struggling with the concept of sin—and the fear of hell that accompanies it—can really damage a person's faith. We need a better understanding of sin; one that reminds us of our accountability and responsibility before the God of Truth, while also grounding us in God's mercy, love, and forgiveness.

1.   What are your questions and concerns regarding the topic of sin?

Chapter 7 "It's About Relationship Not Rules" explained that when we say something is a *sin* it's because it damages our relationship with God; not because it is "breaking the rules." It damages our relationship because it is either directly aimed at hurting God or at hurting those whom God loves (CCC, 1849).

In the Old Testament, sin is defined in two ways. The first is in archery terms: "missing the mark." For instance, when our actions are guided by selfishness rather than *agapic*-love, they miss the mark. The second way sin is described in Scripture is as a "hardness of heart." For example, when we are indifferent to the suffering of others… when we just don't care enough to help someone in need, we are hard-hearted.

2. Can you connect with the definitions of sin in Scripture? Recall a time when your sin resulted from "missing the mark." How about "hardness of heart"?

Catholic Tradition takes these concepts from Old Testament along with the words of Jesus in the Gospels and the writings of St. Paul to expand our understanding of sin.

In the Penitential Rite, we pray:

I confess to almighty God
and to you, my brothers and sisters,
that I have greatly sinned,
in my thoughts and in my words,
in what I have done and in what I have failed to do,
through my fault…

Notice how this prayer recognizes that sin is always committed with intent (*through my fault…*). Additionally, the words of this prayer acknowledge both what Catholic Tradition calls the sins of commission (*doing something wrong*) and the sins of omission (*not doing something that we know we should've done*) – and this happens in thoughts, words, and actions. In all cases, we recognize that there are varying degrees of seriousness, which is why we refer to sin as either venial or mortal (CCC, 1854).

Venial sins include the smaller, less serious acts of sinfulness that often result from the bad habits or laziness. (*I know I should pray, but I don't. I know I shouldn't swear, but I do.*) These are important to recognize because over time they weaken our relationship with God.

As the degree of seriousness increases, Catholic Tradition describes mortal sin. Translated literally, this is a sin which brings a "deadly" or "mortal" blow to one's relationship with God. A mortal sin is a complete, deliberate rejection of God. This is a big deal. We're not just talking about any sin, here. We're talking about a relationship-breaking sin. For it to be considered a "mortal sin" it:

- Must involve "grave matter"
- Must be done with full knowledge.
- Must be done deliberately, with full freedom (CCC, 1859).

It is difficult to broadly and definitively classify anything as a mortal sin because the only one who knows a person's honest level of knowledge, freedom, and intent is God. For instance, consider one of the most disturbing "jobs" during the Holocaust. The Jewish Virtual Library explains that at Auschwitz and several other concentration camps,

> [T]he Nazis established the Sonderkommando, groups of Jewish male prisoners picked for their youth and relative good health whose job was to dispose of corpses from the gas chambers or crematoria. Some did the work to delay their own deaths; some thought they could protect friends and family, and some acted out of mere greed for extra food and money these men sometimes received. The men were forced into this position, with the only alternative being death in the gas chambers or being shot on the spot by an SS guard.[22]

Here we are certainly dealing with a grave matter done with full knowledge, but the prisoners' lack of freedom eliminates the culpability.

Culpability, the degree to which people are morally responsible, can diminish if a sin is committed under duress, whether that pressure comes from oneself or others. Then there are psychological wounds, such as the PTSD of war veterans or mental illness, which likewise limit one's freedom and diminish responsibility.

Suicide is another grave matter that deserves attention. Many of us have been taught that people who commit suicide are going to hell. The reason for this teaching is clear: our life was given to us by God. "We are stewards, not owners, of the life God has entrusted to us. It is not ours to dispose of" (CCC, 2280). If committed with full knowledge and freedom, the intent of suicide is to reject God's gift of life, and rejecting God is a mortal blow to our relationship. However, as the *Catechism* recognizes, "psychological disturbances, anguish, or grave fear of hardship, suffering, or torture can diminish the responsibility of the one committing suicide" (CCC, 2282). As modern psychology has helped us understand that a person who commits suicide is generally not in the right frame of mind, we have come to a more compassionate stance. Suicide is wrong, but "we should not despair of the eternal salvation of persons who have taken

---

[22] The Jewish Virtual Library, "Concentration Camps: The Sonderkommando" by Jacqueline Shields http://www.jewishvirtuallibrary.org/jsource/Holocaust/Sonderkommando.html. Accessed May 7, 2014.

their own lives. By ways known to him alone, God can provide the opportunity for salutary repentance. The Church prays for persons who have taken their own lives" (CCC, 2283).

Is it possible for a person to commit a mortal sin? Absolutely. That possibility is a reflection of the depth of our human freedom. However, not every decision is made with full knowledge, full freedom, and deliberate intent.

Moreover, you know what the remedy is for mortal sin? Reconciliation. Mess up really badly? Take responsibility, seek forgiveness, and make amends. God just wants us to repent and return to him (CCC, 1847).

> Which one of you, having a hundred sheep and losing one of them, does not leave the ninety-nine in the wilderness and go after the one that is lost until he finds it? When he has found it, he lays it on his shoulders and rejoices. And when he comes home, he calls together his friends and neighbors, saying to them, 'Rejoice with me, for I have found my sheep that was lost.' Just so, I tell you, there will be more joy in heaven over one sinner who repents than over ninety-nine righteous people who need no repentance. (Luke 15:4-7)

When Jesus tells the parable of the Lost Sheep, it might be helpful to understand that most shepherds don't leave the 99 to chase after the one. But God does. Because that's just the kind of loving, merciful, life-giving God he is.

Mortal sin is not the end. Rather, it points to a deep, serious need for reconciliation.

Sometimes we need to raise our awareness of the ways in which we do sin. A good *examination of conscience*, which the *Catechism* glossary defines as a "prayerful self–reflection on our words and deeds in the light of the Gospel to determine how we may have sinned against God," can be a tremendous help here. [23]

Other times, we are so aware of our sinfulness that we need to revisit the notion of our inherit goodness of our human dignity alongside the gift of God's grace and mercy. Our Catholic faith affirms both that we are both good and capable of sin.

3. Think about your own attitudes towards sin: When it comes to the topic of moral responsibility and sin, what do you struggle with?

---

[23] The USCCB offers some great resources for examinations of conscience, one uses the Ten Commandments, another Catholic Social Teaching. They also offer different ones for children, young adults, singles, and married persons. Visit http://www.usccb.org/prayer-and-worship/sacraments-and-sacramentals/penance/examinations-of-conscience.cfm. (Accessed June 2, 2014).

4. When it comes to the topic of moral responsibility and sin, what do you need to hear more about: examining your conscience to take responsibility or God's grace and mercy?

5. Regarding your answer to number 4, what do you plan to do to make that happen?

# Chapter 15

# Joy

Rejoice in the Lord always. I shall say it again: rejoice!
(Phillipians 4:4)

Scripture mentions joy (or rejoice) over 400 times.[24]  Joy is a contentment, confidence, and hope that resonates deep within.  Joy fosters a big-picture outlook encompassing the growth and well-being of one's body, mind, and soul.  Joy is enduring. Joy has a spiritual dimension to it – as if it is the very experience of one's soul taking delight.  Joy is infused with love and gratitude.[25]

1.  How else would you describe joy?

---

[24] According to *Strongest of Strong's Exhaustive Concordance of the Bible*, variations of joy (joyous, joyful, etc.) appear 201 times; variations of rejoice (rejoicing, rejoiced, etc.) appear in Scripture 226 times.  (James Strong.  Grand Rapids: Zondervan, 2001, pages 557 and 875-876.)

[25] The focus on joy in this chapter aligns with happiness.  Depending on how you define it, the two terms are more similar than different.  Many of us use the words happiness and joy interchangeably; most dictionaries define the words quite similarly.  Scripture references both terms.  The *Catechism* notes how Scripture speaks of happiness: "true happiness is not found in riches or well-being, in human fame or power, or in any human achievement - however beneficial it may be - such as science, technology, and art, or indeed in any creature, but in God alone, the source of every good and of all love" (CCC, 1723). Recent *New York Times* bestseller, *The Happiness Project* by Gretchen Rubin (2009) explores a multitude of the philosophical and theological commentaries on what happiness is all about.  For many, "happiness" conjures images of immediate, transitory, situational pleasure. Throughout her book, Rubin cites philosophers and theologians throughout the ages who offer a variety of definitions and descriptions about what happiness is and is not. Rubin's expression of happiness is aligned with the understanding of joy expressed in this chapter.

2.  What are the times in your life that stand out for you as an experience of joy?

Joy is given to us by God; it is the awareness of the presence of God. The poet Elizabeth Barrett Browning (1806-1861) wrote:

*Earth's crammed with heaven.*
*And every common bush afire with God;*
*But only he who sees, takes off his shoes –*
*The rest sit round it and pluck blackberries.*

Earth is crammed with heaven, and joy permeates life. But only those who see it take off their shoes. How often do we see—or appreciate—joy?

3.  Comment on how well you see (or appreciate) joy in your daily life.

4.  Who do you know that emanates joy? How do you feel when you are around this person?

In many ways, joy as much about having an *increased awareness* about the presence of God as it is about changing our perspective on otherwise mediocre (or downright annoying) events in life.

If we allow it, joy can become a way of life.

~~~~~

*One year my New Year's resolution was joy. I decided to work on having an increased awareness. I challenged myself to embrace the smiles which my kids bring me as opportunities for joy. That required me to stop and really see and appreciate the smiles when they happened. Instead of complaining about the mess, I reveled in the opportunity to vacuum my carseat-free RAV4 and liberate it from the Cheerios, Chex, and raisins imbedded in the back seat.*

~~~~~

*When I make the time for a favorite hobby – crafting and painting – I am filled with joy. It allows me to create something new and fun, while using my imagination. So, so much fun! Joy.*

~~~~~

*Once, I found myself with an extra 25 minutes between my appointments, so I called my husband, coordinated meeting at the park near his work, and packed a picnic lunch. The unexpected fun was delightful. Joy.*

~~~~~

*I have white tiles with "supposedly" white grout on my kitchen floor. Really scrubbing that grout is a hands-and-knees chore that I've been avoiding for two solid years. But I resolved to embrace it and look for the joy. A good scrub brush, a bucket of water, a decent cleaning agent, some towels, and a couple of hours, along with a lot of elbow grease and the grout went from black to off-white. I not only found joy in a job well done, but in the "lather, rinse, repeat" mode of repetitive cleaning, I had a lot of time to simply think and reflect – which in and of itself is a total bonus. My wrists hurt quite a bit afterwards, but with a focus on joy, I was able to acknowledge the pain and still get excited every time I walked into the kitchen, basking in the glory of sparkling white floors.*

~~~~~

From the standpoint of faith, this focus on joy helps us tune into the presence of God in daily life. It reminds us of the virtue of hope and maintaining a proper perspective on what does and does not matter.

Joy is available to you. You need only to see it.

5. Is there anything you feel called to do differently? What can you do to increase your awareness and see the joy in your life this week?

6. Come back to this question after you spend some time actively seeking joy in your everyday life.

- How did it go?  What worked well?  Where did you struggle?

- How did actively seeking joy impact your faith life?

# Chapter 16

# Regret and Remorse

⚝

With two young boys, I make it a point to overhear things, particularly playtime interactions, car ride conversations, and whatever they are watching on the television. So it's not like I was intentionally watching an episode of *Lego Ninjago*, it's just that it actually captured more of my attention than I would like to admit.

In the episode "Wrong Place, Wrong Time," the bad guy (Lord Garmadon) wishes that the good guys (Ninjas) never existed, so he goes back in time to make it so. As the save-the-day Ninjas prepare to follow, they are warned by their mentor (Sensei Wu) that *if they change anything, they change everything.*

The episode reminded me of a conversation I had with my Grandmom in one of her last visits to my house.

> *"Kid, there were some difficult times in my life. I'll tell you, 1936 was hard – extremely hard. But let me just say this: I have no regrets. Isn't that something? At my age: 83 years old, and no regrets." She paused and looked me in the eye, "Can you say the same for yourself? Do you have any regrets?"*

> *I looked at her with tears in my eyes. "No. I can't say that. I do have a huge regret. My first marriage was a huge mistake. I regret that it ever happened. I regret making that choice. With every fiber of my being, I regret that."*

> *Grandmom does this vice grip pinch of my upper arm with surprising strength for a feeble old lady and tells me, "I'm not saying I never made any mistakes. Kid, I made plenty of mistakes. Plenty. Ask anyone. I'm talking regrets."*

> *"I know, Grandmom. I do. I wish it wasn't a regret. But it is."*

> *"I hope one day you change your mind. I hope one day you can get to my age and say that you have no regrets. Because that's really something."*

Grandmom died the following December, still having no regrets.

So as I sat in the dining room, sipping my tea and finishing breakfast, I hear Sensei Wu warn the Ninjas that *if you change anything, you change everything.* And I finally got it.

Regret and remorse are two different things. I have sincere *remorse* for the series of well-intentioned, yet ill-informed decisions that led to one of the lowest point in my life. I am deeply sorry. The turmoil, crisis, depression... I am very sorry. But Grandmom was talking about the kind of regret that wipes the event off the face of the earth. And as Sensei Wu said, *change anything, change everything.* Would I be willing to change *everything?*

*My husband... my boys... my friends... my community... my personal and spiritual growth... No. I don't want to risk changing who, and what, and where I am now. So I'm making peace with how I got here.*

I'm getting closer to telling Grandmom, "No. I don't have any regrets." And I hear her saying, "That's good, kid. That's *great!*" (Though, the imaginary vice grip hurts a lot less than the real one.)

1. When you think about the mistakes you have made in your life, is your attitude towards them more of regret or remorse? Why? Has your attitude shifted over time? Explain.

2. Identify some of the *goodness* that has occurred in your life in the wake of the brokenness of mistakes, struggles, suffering, and evil.

## Divine Providence and the Scandal of Evil

Reflecting on *some of the goodness that has occurred in the wake of suffering* gives us hope. We get ourselves into trouble, however, when we use phrases like "everything happens for a reason" or "it was meant to be" to convey this hope. Imagine a rape survivor or a Holocaust survivor hearing "everything happens for a reason." The expression falsely implies that God caused the evil to occur so that the good would follow.

Our faith certainly gives us hope in the face of suffering and death, yet Church teaching explicitly rejects the idea that God would cause evil to occur so that we can learn and grow.

In the section on Divine Providence and the Scandal of Evil (CCC, 309-314), the *Catechism* lays it out:

- God is all good
- God *does not cause* evil to happen
- Evil happens

Quoting St. Augustine, the *Catechism* explains:

> For almighty God...because he is supremely good, would never allow any evil whatsoever to exist in his works if he were not so all-powerful and good as to cause good to emerge from evil itself. (CCC, 311)

God did not cause the bad things to happen to you, me, or anyone else. Theologically, everything *does not* happen for a reason.

A more truthful expression might be: When life gives you lemons, God makes the best divine lemonade you could possibly imagine. We all have our own story of divine lemonade.

~~~~~

*Heidi and Cody struggled with infertility for years. During the years of heartbreak and loss, they struggled in their relationship with God. They tried, but were unable to find God working through any of it. And then God put it in their hearts to adopt—specifically through foster care—a direction that God made very clear. Of the three children they adopted, two came from particularly difficult family background situations.*

*"By being adoptive parents, we feel that God has given us the awesome privilege of playing a role in many different lives. We are able to help our children create a different arc...a different trajectory for their lives—for their futures—so that the patterns that got their birth parents into the dysfunctional situations that they were in (by the grace of God) won't be repeated in our children's lives. And if our children do things right, perhaps that difference will continue in their children's lives, and their grandchildren's lives, and so on. We see all of this as a privilege – the privilege of being used by God for this specific purpose. We get to do this for Him. We get to help create His Kingdom on Earth through the lives of these children we have adopted."*

~~~~~

God didn't cause any of this pain and suffering, but He did transform it. God—and only God—can transform evil into something good.

3. Recall some of the messages of *hope in the midst of darkness* that you have given and/or received. How do these messages compare with the Church's teaching on Divine Providence and Evil?

4. Tell one of your own stories of "divine lemonade."

5. Think of someone who is going through a difficult time right now; contact them and offer a message of hope that honors this teaching.

# Chapter 17

# Forgiveness

My youngest was having difficulty with the kid across the street, whom he considers his best friend. Over the course of several days, feelings had been hurt in both directions and neither boy was handling it well. Each perpetuated the cycle of my-feelings-are-hurt-so-I'm-going-to-hurt-your-feelings.

When our children make mistakes, we teach them to do three important things to assist in the process of forgiveness:

1) Take Responsibility *for your role in the situation*
2) Seek Forgiveness *from whomever you have hurt*
3) Fix It – *do what you can to work on repairing any damage you've done*

Forgiveness is hard, and it's hard for different people for different reasons. Everyone has that one aspect that they struggle with, whether it's forgiving oneself, forgiving others, or seeking forgiveness.

So when discussing why that cycle of *my-feelings-are-hurt-so-I'm-going-to-hurt-your-feelings* was wrong (and unhelpful, and hurtful), it didn't surprise me when my son started crying. But instead of assuming, I compassionately asked *"Why are you crying?"*

*"Because I know what I did was wrong and I'm ashamed."*

*"Oh honey. No. That's not what I want. That's not what God wants."*

## Forgiveness of Self

Shame breaks forgiveness. It stops us from learning, growing, healing, and loving. Shame paralyzes us in the first part of the process *Take Responsibility*, and it brings its friend *fear* to prevent us from moving on to the second part *Seeking Forgiveness* from whoever you've hurt… so that we might as well forget about making any progress on the third part *Fixing It*. That paralysis not helpful.

For many of us, the hardest part about forgiveness is honestly forgiving ourselves.

- How could I have been so stupid?
- How could I have made such an awful mistake?

Some wonder: *can* we forgive ourselves? Isn't it up to God to forgive us? To that I'd respond: certainly. God is ultimately the one who forgives. But Jesus offered extra clarification here: we're not supposed to be judging and condemning ourselves in the first place. Recall the story of the woman caught in the act of adultery:

> "Teacher, this woman was caught in the very act of committing adultery. Now in the law, Moses commanded us to stone such women. So what do you say?" They said this to test him, so that they could have some charge to bring against him. Jesus bent down and began to write on the ground with his finger. But when they continued asking him, he straightened up and said to them, "Let the one among you who is without sin be the first to throw a stone at her." Again he bent down and wrote on the ground. And in response, they went away one by one, beginning with the elders. So he was left alone with the woman before him. Then Jesus straightened up and said to her, "Woman, where are they? Has no one condemned you?" She replied, "No one, sir." Then Jesus said, "Neither do I condemn you. Go, [and] from now on do not sin anymore." (John 8:4-11)

Look closely at the final words Jesus said to the woman, "Neither do I condemn you. Go, and from now on do not sin anymore." God is a God of love and life. Shame and condemnation are not what God wants for our lives. Rather, Jesus tells us to learn and grow from this experience (*sin no more*) and go on your way–move forward in life with love.

1. Evaluate yourself with regards to *forgiveness of self*. How well do you practice this? What do you struggle with? Do you need to forgive yourself?

2. What encouragement do you need to hear when it comes to *forgiveness of self*?

## Forgiveness of Others

Jesus speaks most clearly on the topic of forgiving others, particularly telling us to love our enemies (Matthew 5:44, Luke 6:27) and forgive seven times seven times (Matthew 18:21-22, Luke 17:4). Taken as a whole, Jesus' message of forgiveness is radical: We are to be people of love and reconciliation, not people of hate and vengeance.

There is no wiggle room in Christianity when it comes to hatred and vengeance. Most Christians agree with this in theory, but have difficulty when putting it in to practice, especially in instances of abuse, particularly when it comes to the teaching about retaliation.

> You have heard that it was said, "An eye for an eye and a tooth for a tooth." But I say to you, offer no resistance to one who is evil. When someone strikes you on (your) right cheek, turn the other one to him as well. (Matthew 5:38-39)

At no point in the Gospels does Jesus preach a message contrary to love. Abuse is not love. So to interpret this passage in a way that encourages someone to endure ongoing, continued abuse would be a gross misinterpretation. Still, what is Jesus saying here?

Contemporary readers usually imagine these "strikes" as a fist fight. Actually, in biblical times it was common for a Roman/male "master" to backhand-slap an inferior (slaves, wives, children, Jews). A backhand-slap means to use the back of your hand, not your palm, to slap someone. The intent of this "strike" was more to degrade the inferior than to hurt. In that culture, the left hand was only used for "unclean tasks," so this backhand slap necessitated the master's right hand on the inferior's right cheek. Most people chose to respond with one of two extremes: either let it alone (submitting to the abuse) or fight back (with eye-for-an-eye violence), but while addressing a group of people who are used to being degraded, Jesus offers a third way. He instructs them to be subversive with creative non-violence. By literally, physically turning and offering "the other (left) cheek," the master can no longer backhand-slap; the only possible "hit" would be with a fist to the left cheek. In that society, only equals fought with fists; thus "turning the other cheek" was an act of defiance that honored human dignity.[26]

Using love and respect for human dignity to guide forgiveness, let us also explore what it means to forgive a person who is unrepentant.

~~~~~

*As a child, Grace was molested by an uncle who lived with her large Catholic family. The abuse continued for years, but she never told anyone. As an adult, when Grace*

---

[26] Protestant biblical scholar, Walter Wink (d. 2012) offers this exegesis of "turn the other cheek" in *The Powers That Be* (Doubleday, 1998). On their website, Christian Peacemaker Teams offers a link to Wink's text, which can be found at http://www.cpt.org/files/BN%20-%20Jesus'%20Third%20Way.pdf. Accessed March 20, 2014.

*recalls her story, she recognizes that though the abuse remained a secret, there were signs of extreme self-loathing that permeated her childhood and adolescence, lasting into much of her adulthood. Grace's uncle had long since passed away, never acknowledging or apologizing for his actions. She knew that she needed forgiveness and healing in this area of her life. However, when Grace talked about forgiveness, she focused on her need to forgive her molester. "I struggle with that, because it seems like saying that I'm okay with what he did. And I'm not."*

~~~~~

When Jesus spoke to his disciples about forgiveness, he was calling them to reconcile, love, and be at peace with one another. True *reconciliation* is only possible between two people who come together in mutual respect to make amends. *Forgiveness,* however, isn't dependent on anyone else's actions or words.

As part of a series on emotions, PBS did a segment called "Understanding Forgiveness." In it, researchers offer some great insights and descriptions of what forgiveness is and is not from the perspective of social psychologists:

> Forgiveness, at a minimum, is a decision to let go of the desire for revenge and ill-will toward the person who wronged you. It may also include feelings of goodwill toward the other person.
>
> **Forgiveness is not the same as reconciliation.** Forgiveness is one person's inner response to another's perceived injustice. Reconciliation requires both parties working together. Forgiveness is something that is entirely up to you.
>
> **Forgiveness is not forgetting.** "Forgive and forget" seem to go together. However, the process of forgiving involves you acknowledging the wrong that was done to you, reflecting on it, and deciding how you want to think about it. Focusing on forgetting a wrong might lead to denying or suppressing feelings about it, which is not the same as forgiveness. Forgiveness has taken place when you can remember the wrong that was done without feeling resentment or a desire to pursue revenge. Sometimes, after we get to this point, we may forget about some of the wrongs people have done to us. But we don't have to forget in order to forgive.
>
> **Forgiveness is not condoning or excusing.** Forgiveness does not minimize, justify, or excuse the wrong that was done. Forgiveness also does not mean denying the harm and the feelings that the injustice produced. And forgiveness does not mean putting yourself in a position

to be harmed again. You can forgive someone and still take healthy steps to protect yourself. [27]

Forgiveness is about letting go of the anger, hatred, and desire for revenge.

~~~~~

*Grace realized that she did not hold on to hatred, anger, or a desire for revenge for her uncle. She did, however, hold on to anger and hatred for herself. When she released the idea that she was expected to "be okay" with the molestation, Grace began to heal.*

~~~~~

3. Evaluate yourself with regards to *forgiveness of others*. How well do you practice this? What do you struggle with? Is there someone you need to forgive?

4. What encouragement do you need to hear when it comes to *forgiveness of others*?

**Seeking Forgiveness**

Sometimes we have a hard time with actually seeking forgiveness. Doing so requires vulnerability.

- Am I too proud or angry to take responsibility for my role?
- Will my apology be received?

---

[27] The segment "Understanding Forgiveness" was part of the PBS a series called "This Emotional Life." In it, PBS cites psychologist Sonja Lyubomirsky and her book *The How of Happiness* (Penguin Press, 2007). The explanation of forgiveness is available on the PBS website at http://www.pbs.org/thisemotionallife/topic/forgiveness/understanding-forgiveness. (Accessed March 20, 2014.)

- Will I be made to feel worse than I already do? (Is that even possible?)
- What will they think of me?
- Does apologizing make me look weak?

Jesus told us to make peace with one another before coming to the altar (Matthew 5:23-25).  This peace is a matter of love and wholeness.  We are told to reconcile with one another, and we are also invited to receive the healing grace in the Sacrament of Reconciliation.  And what a gift of grace it is!  The peace!

So while yes, it is scary to be vulnerable, Christian discipleship is about being real, taking that risk, and living in love with one another.

5. Evaluate yourself with regards to *seeking forgiveness*.  How well do you practice this?  What do you struggle with?  Is there someone you need to seek forgiveness from?

6. What encouragement do you need to hear when it comes to *seeking forgiveness*?

7. Overall—in any of the three categories—what has been your most significant experience with forgiveness?

# Chapter 18

# Theology of the Body

⟁

In September of 1979, within a year of the start of his papacy, Saint John Paul II began a series of talks at his Wednesday audiences, which lasted through November of 1984. These 129 lectures were compiled together and became known as the "Theology of the Body." Theology of the Body offers a renewed, life-giving way for understanding sex and sexual morality, and this life-giving vision lends itself to a whole way of understanding all "bodily" interaction. The lectures begin with the meaning and dignity of the human person at Creation, and then explore the implications.[28]

1. Think about how you learned about sex and sexual morality. Was it part of a larger vision of the human person or was it more along the lines of a list of rules? Explain.

The concept of human dignity has been discussed in several chapters throughout this book. As Christians, we have a vision of what it means to be human. We were created

---

[28] There were several interruptions to the Wednesday lectures on Theology of the Body, when attention was given to other topics, such as the "Year of Holy Redemption" in 1983. The content of the 129 lectures is available online through the USCCB website (http://www.usccb.org/issues-and-action/marriage-and-family/natural-family-planning/catholic-teaching/theology-of-the-body.cfm Accessed June 5, 2014). Christopher West is one of the most popular authors, speakers, and teachers on the topic of Theology of the Body. He offers a paragraph-by-paragraph explanation of each of the lectures in the series in *Theology of the Body Explained: A Commentary on John Paul II's Man and Woman He Created Them* (Pauline Books, First Edition 2003, Revised Edition 2007). In addition to several additional books and study guides on this topic, West offers the *Theology of the Body Institute* (http://www.tobinstitute.org/), which is committed to teaching about this important work.

in the image and likeness of God, which gives us each a unique specialness: we are the image of God in body and soul. It is this very nature of our creation that calls us to love one another as God loves us. In all we say and all we do, we are called to respect this inherent human dignity in ourselves and others.

In creating us and designing our way of being with each other, God has a vision for what is supposed to be expressed and experienced in sex, and God's vision is phenomenal. God intended for the sexual aspects of our bodies to be a way for two people to say: "We love each other enough to become one."[29]

> The fact that they become one flesh is a powerful bond established by the Creator. Through it they discover their own humanity, both in its original unity, and in the duality of a mysterious mutual attraction. (*TOB*, 10:2)

As Genesis 2:4 says "two become one," a Theology of the Body understands that union goes well beyond what happens physically. Through sexual intercourse, two become one physically, intellectually, emotionally, and spiritually. It is as if we are saying:

> *"I love you so much that I give my whole self*
> *– body, mind, and soul –*
> *to you completely, without any reservation."*

This complete union involves a total gift of self – mutually given and received in all four senses of love (*agape, philia, storge,* and *eros,* from Chapter 8). This intense message is communicated with the body, in the body, through the body – it's a bodily language. The body was designed by God to be truthful.

In honestly and truthfulness, think about who you trust with your deepest, darkest secrets. In fact, what would it take for you to open yourself up to someone and be totally vulnerable – emotionally naked – with your whole life? In God's vision and design, through sex, the body communicates with exactly *that* level of vulnerability and openness.

2. Who do you "*trust with your deepest, darkest secrets*"? Male or female, in *philia* or *eros,* with whom are you able to be vulnerable?

---

[29] I wrote about the Theology of the Body in a series of features in Our Sunday Visitor Curriculum Division's high school textbook series. These "Honoring the Body" features can be found in Course 1: *Jesus the Word* (2011) and Course 2: *Son of the Living God* (2011). The feature that specifically addresses this vision of sex is called "One Body," and can be found in Course 1: *Jesus the Word*, pages 28-29.

*The body communicates with exactly that level of vulnerability and openness,* except when it doesn't. The body was not designed to lie (which is why lie detectors work, why we sweat when we're nervous, and why it's so difficult to suppress laughter). So if a person engages in this gift of oneself, but it *does* have reservations—for whatever reason—it needs to protect itself. To do so, the body begins to numb itself to vulnerability and trust. By numbing itself, the body allows itself to be used as an object... as a means to an end. While in and of itself, this is a problematic disrespect of human dignity, this also means that when a person *does* enter into a loving union in the Sacrament of Marriage, the damage does not immediately and miraculously undo itself.

3. Think about the "disrespect of human dignity" that occurs when "the body allows itself to be used as a means to an end." While this chapter focuses on this dynamic occurring in sexual encounters, a Theology of the Body rejects the objectification of humankind in every circumstance. Have you ever been "used as an object"? As you consider your answer, think about interactions in the workplace... interactions within your friend or family relationships...

4. Along the same lines, think of a time when you used another person as an object... as a means to an end. Did you disrespect the humanity of the cashier at the store? Did you disrespect the humanity of an employee... of a family member... of a friend? Recall one or two examples. How could you have handled the situation differently?

What does it take to rebuild trust? What does it take to rebuild enough trust to be emotionally naked and vulnerable? A lot of healing over time. We know this emotionally within any relationships that have suffered a blow to trust. Our body knows this as well.

A Theology of the Body recognizes the validity of bodily knowledge as part of the goodness of God's creation and design.

Sex is a bodily gift of one's very self, involving as much emotional nakedness as physical. Tremendous openness and vulnerability are needed to be able to truthfully express "*I love you so much that I give my whole self—body, mind, and soul—to you completely, without any reservation.*" When both husband and wife give themselves to each other *without reservation*, it is a wonderful, beautiful, incredible act of intimacy, and it feels great.

5. What encouraging words or wisdom can you take from Theology of the Body for your own life? What insight can you work on putting into practice this week?

# Chapter 19

# Obsession or Appreciation

⟁

*Even though I'm not a huge TV watcher, there are some shows I really enjoy. One night, we were watching a really good episode of Grey's Anatomy on the DVR. Some sports game had run long and pushed the start time back by 10 or 15 minutes, but the DVR was only set to record an extra 3 minutes. The show cut off in the middle of the climax.*

*I start screaming "No!" with pained lamentation worthy of Job. I'm screaming, yelling, and cursing the TV, the sporting event, and all the people, places, and things involved.*

*My husband responds simply, "That's disappointing." And after watching me rant and rave for a few minutes, he finally says, "You really need to calm down. It's just a television show. It's not the end of the world."*

*There was absolutely no defense I could muster for my over-the-top reaction. I got annoyed with my husband's dismissive attitude, but loathe as I was to admit it, he was right. Instead of being appropriately disappointed, I was more along the lines of devastated…over a TV show.*

*The incident clued me in to some obsessive behavior that I was neither aware of nor proud of.*

~ ~ ~ ~ ~

Call it addiction, attachment, a compulsion, a fixation, an obsession, dependence, or a need… The over-the-top reaction to some desired thing is an issue.

It's not a new issue. In 1989, when Billy Joel sang "I Go to Extremes," he was hitting on a common struggle.[30] Philosophers and theologians have written about it – from Plato, to Sacred Scripture, to St. Thomas Aquinas, to contemporary spiritual writers such as Anthony De Mello. What we're talking about is the virtue of temperance.

Temperance, prudence (wisdom), fortitude (courage), and justice are the four cardinal virtues. The word cardinal comes from the Latin word for "hinge." These four virtues are hinges upon which the door of the moral life swings.

---

[30] Billy Joel, "I Go to Extremes," Storm Front. Columbia Records, 1989.

Temperance is moderation in one's actions, thoughts, or feelings. It's the practice of self-control and restraint. The virtue of temperance is focused on moving us beyond an all-or-nothing approach to a place of balance. (See CCC, 1809.)

Each person has their own successes and struggles with it – everyone has their thing. Consider the following topics and feel free to add your own:

- Money
- Power
- Technology: Cell phone, email, Facebook, Twitter, txt msg, internet…
- Media: TV shows, movies, news, celebrity gossip, video games, books, magazines…
- Consumption: food, sweets, caffeine, alcohol, drugs, smoking…
- Sports: sports teams (spectator or athlete), exercise, fitness…
- Interpersonal: sex, dating, relationships, wedding planning…
- Shopping: clothes, shoes, purses, cars, toys…
- Beauty: hair, nails, makeup…
- Perfection: perfect diet, perfect mom, perfect dad, perfect house, perfect organization, perfect decisions…

Identifying the areas of success with the virtue of temperance are as important as identifying our areas of struggle. Our successes give us more than an affirmation; they provide us with an understanding of what a healthy attitude towards something we enjoy looks and feels like.

1. When it comes to the virtue of temperance, own your areas of success:
   - I enjoy and have a healthy appreciation of _____ without becoming overly attached to it.

2. When it comes to the virtue of temperance, recognize your areas of weakness.
   - I struggle with moderation when it comes to _____.

After identifying your areas of struggle, the next step is to make a conscious decision to develop a better practice of temperance. As your attitude shifts from obsession to healthy appreciation, you will notice more *freedom*. You no longer *have* to do something, rather you can choose to do it or not.

How do we get from obsession to temperance? The Christian tradition has a strong history in the practice of asceticism, which is the disciplined practice of abstaining from worldly pleasures. (Asceticism is often confused with the similar sounding term "aesthetics," which is the branch of philosophy dealing with art and beauty.)

The practice of self-denial in asceticism isn't virtuous in and of itself. Rather, it is a time-tested way to remove all distractions from one's life so as to focus more fully and completely on the Way, the Truth, and the Light that is God.

For example, take the practice of "giving something up" for Lent. And for the sake of argument, let's say that "something" was candy. Candy is not evil. Nor is avoiding candy virtuous. But if your attitude towards candy goes beyond "healthy appreciation…" If you have a hard time practicing self-control around an open bowl of candy… If your desire for candy is over-the-top… You might consider the ascetic practice of self-denial to break the dependency on candy.

Break the attachment to whatever it is that you give an undue amount of focus, attention, and energy to. Because again, it's not about the thing. It's about the place and position of power we are giving that thing in our lives. It's in this way that practicing the virtue of temperance (and engaging in the practice of asceticism) helps us to honor the First Commandment.

I am the Lord your God. You shall have no other gods besides me.
(Exodus 20:2-3)

Few of us have golden calves that we are tempted to worship, but we do have smartphones. It's the things we put in the "#1" position in our life, the things we give undue amounts of our energy and attention to… It's the things we struggle with practicing the virtue of temperance that become stumbling blocks for the First Commandment.

Some addictions are so unhealthy and all-consuming that they require complete abstinence for the long-term. However, that is not the case for everything. For example, consider one person's struggle with perfectionism:

~~~~~

*I'm an "everything has its place" sort of person. Focusing on temperance has helped me realize that while clean and straightened is good, it's not nearly as important as being fully present to my children. Organization has its place in helping my life function. But it cannot take center stage over-and-above quality time with my family.*

~~~~~

It wouldn't be helpful to forsake all cleaning and organization efforts. The better solution is to forsake the addiction to perfection and live a more balanced life. The goal is to go from addiction to appreciation.

3. What insight from this chapter really resonates with you? Explain.

4. Identify one area of struggle that you will make a conscious decision to develop a better practice of temperance. Why this one?

5. What steps will you take?

# Chapter 20

# Liturgy Is Not a Spectator Sport

When Catholics use the word liturgy, we mean to indicate a formal, public work of prayer. There are Eucharistic liturgies (like at Sunday Mass) and non-Eucharistic liturgies (like at a Baptism outside of a Mass). The word "liturgy" comes from a Greek term that originally meant a "public work" or a "work done on behalf of the people." But this work of prayer isn't something that was ever intended to be done "for" us on our behalf, while we sit back and watch. In Christian tradition, liturgy "means the participation of the People of God in 'the work of God'" (CCC, 1069).

As the People of God, all of us are expected to actively participate in liturgy. Liturgy is not a spectator sport.

1. To what degree do you participate in liturgy? To what degree do you approach liturgy as a passive spectator?

While all People of God are called to "full, conscious, and active participation" in liturgical celebrations (CCC, 1141), all of us do not have the same function.

> For as in one body we have many parts, and all the parts do not have the same function. (Romans 12:4)

Priests and deacons have a special role in service to the community, particularly when it comes to liturgy and Sacraments. The way in which we understand *leadership*, however, has a tremendous impact on how we understand the role of the priest and the responsibility of the faithful in both liturgy and Sacraments.

2.  Think about the *best* teacher, leader, or boss you've ever worked with. Who was it? What was it that made them such a good leader? On the flip-side, think about that experience with someone who was a rather *poor* leader, teacher, or boss? What were the characteristics or behaviors that made it so?

Good leaders take the time, effort, and energy to teach and empower people. They encourage creativity and appreciate individual strengths. Good leaders facilitate growth, often by allowing people to make mistakes and learn from them. They practice good communication skills, both in expressing themselves and in understanding others. They care about their people, and their people know it. Good leaders value responsibility, honesty, integrity, and hard work. They offer assistance when it is needed. They work at creating atmospheres of mutual respect. They approach leadership as form of service as they maintain a big-picture sense of mission and vision.

On the other hand, we find it easy to complain about "poor" leaders who tend to micro-manage every aspect of people's work. Their style of leadership makes people feel small and insignificant – like a replaceable cog in the wheel. Poor leaders control others through fear or manipulation and are often self-centered, arrogant, or egotistical. Whether they are narrow-minded or overly strict, their leadership style diminishes both freedom and creativity.

Notice this list describes a "poor" leader, not a "bad" leader with malicious intent or "evil" dictators.

## Good Shepherd Leadership

We speak of the priests and bishops in our Church as shepherding the flock. Look at the way in which Scripture uses the image of a Shepherd for explaining who God is and how God relates to us. Three specific passages come to mind: Psalm 23, the Parable of the Lost Sheep (Matthew 18:12-14, Luke 15:1-7), and John 10:1-16.

The Lord is my shepherd, I shall not want. He makes me lie down in green pastures; he leads me beside still waters; he restores my soul. He leads me in right paths for his name's sake. Even though I walk through the darkest valley, I fear no evil; for you are with me; your rod and your staff— they comfort me. (Psalm 23:1-4)

Which one of you, having a hundred sheep and losing one of them, does not leave the ninety-nine in the wilderness and go after the one that is lost until he finds it? When he has found it, he lays it on his shoulders and rejoices. And when he comes home, he calls together his friends and neighbors, saying to them, "Rejoice with me, for I have found my sheep that was lost." Just so, I tell you, there will be more joy in heaven over one sinner who repents than over ninety-nine righteous persons who need no repentance. (Luke 15:4-7)

I am the good shepherd. The good shepherd lays down his life for the sheep. The hired hand, who is not the shepherd and does not own the sheep, sees the wolf coming and leaves the sheep and runs away—and the wolf snatches them and scatters them. The hired hand runs away because a hired hand does not care for the sheep. (John 10:11-13)

The Good Shepherd loves, cares for, and leads his sheep; he does not *rule over* them. He protects them and looks for them when they are lost. The Good Shepherd is the model for leadership that Jesus gives us. It is a model of guidance, not micro-management.

## Liturgy and Sacraments with the Good Shepherd

The model of leadership that Jesus provides in the Good Shepherd is one that encourages, cultivates, and nurtures our participation in the public work of prayer in liturgy. The Good Shepherd also invites our participation in the gift of grace in the Sacraments.

The Sacraments are not magical things that happen to us. One way to think about the empowering leadership of the Good Shepherd is to think of liturgy and Sacraments with what's been called a bumper-sticker theology:

> *Without us, God won't.*
> *Without God, we can't.*

Without us, God won't. Jesus is the Good Shepherd. He does not micromanage our experience of faith. He invites us to participate with him in the transforming power of God's grace.

Without God, we can't. We need God's grace. We cannot do it without God's help.

The Good Shepherd wants to lead you. But to really make it work, you've got to want it too.

3.  When it comes to our understanding of liturgy and Sacraments, it is very important that we check in with our expectations: Do you expect the priest to micromanage our experience and make it happen for us? Or do you enter into the experience of liturgy and Sacraments expecting the leadership of the Good Shepherd who empowers us to participate in receiving God's grace?

4.  What insight from this chapter spoke to you? Why?

5.  What change(s) do you feel called to make? Why? What steps will you take to make that happen?

# Chapter 21

# Eucharist

⟁

The Eucharist has a unique place in our faith as the "Sacrament of sacraments" (CCC, 1211).

1. Focus on your own experience of receiving Eucharist. Was there a time that you yearned for the Eucharist? Was there a time that the Eucharist brought healing or love? What does receiving the Eucharist mean for you?

The Gospels of Matthew, Mark, and Luke describe how Jesus gave us the gift of himself at the Last Supper.

> Then he took the bread, said the blessing, broke it, and gave it to them, saying, "This is my body, which will be given for you; do this in memory of me." And likewise the cup after they had eaten, saying, "This cup is the new covenant in my blood, which will be shed for you. (Luke 22:19-20)

The real, true presence of Christ is given to us in the Eucharist.

Even by calling it Eucharist, we recognize this presence as a gift for which we thank God. The Greek word *eucharistein* means "to give thanks" (CCC, 1328). When we call it Holy Communion, we also recognize how this gift of Divine presence unites us in community with Christ and one another.

The gift of Christ's presence in the Eucharist is so profound that the Church refers to it as "the source and summit of our faith" (*LG* 11; cf. *CCC*, 1324). The word "source" refers to the beginning or place of origin, and the "summit" refers to the highest point of aspiration. The Eucharist is both where our faith begins as well as where it reaches its fullest expression.

~~~~~

*Kathleen recalls yearning for the Eucharist as a child: "At a school Mass, as I walked up to receive, my heart began to beat faster and faster. I was so eager and excited for my turn. I was going to get Jesus! The priest put the Host into my hands, and I was overjoyed. Here was Jesus in my hands, coming to me! Father must have noticed because he patted me on the wrist."*

~~~~~

*Alicia and her husband were married for 17 years before their marriage was convalidated. "I did not receive Communion for all that time. When my convalidation finally took place, I was so ready to receive. I just wanted to take all the Jesus I could get. I just wanted to reach out and take the whole Ciborium full of hosts from Father. But more than that, for a very long time afterwards (and every once in a while, still to this day) upon receiving communion I would weep uncontrollably. I am not upset... I am at total peace. I am just so overcome with love... so humbled that Jesus died for me, and this is His body. He is with me. I cannot explain it. I cannot stop it from happening. All I know is that is it a gift."*[31]

~~~~~

*Mo explains "When I receive the Eucharist, I am nourished. Physically, my spirit leaps. When I am privileged with the responsibility of serving as an Extraordinary Minister of the Eucharistic, the spirit in me touches the spirit in each person I serve. It is such a gift."*

~~~~~

*For Donna, "The phrase 'my cup runneth over' so clearly describes my emotions. I feel love pouring out from the Lord through me each time I said, 'The body of Christ.'"*

~~~~~

2. How do you experience the gift of God's presence—the Eucharist—in your life?

---

[31] Couples who are not married in the Church, but want their union to be validated by the Church at a later date seek "convalidation." There are a variety of reasons why a couple might not have their marriage officially recognized by the Church upon the initial exchange of vows. Many (though not all) circumstances involve divorce and require annulment.

When we call the Eucharist a gift, we recognize that it is a gift *from God*, given *to us*. This powerful gift of grace has the potential to transform us, but we need to receive it.

Watch how Jesus invites the apostles into this transformation in the Gospel of John. Where the other Gospels describe institution of the Eucharist at the Last Supper, John provides us with the foot washing (John 13:1-20). It is as though John skips right to the meaning of the Eucharist by describing this act of humble service.

> Do you realize what I have done for you? You call me "teacher" and "master," and rightly so, for indeed I am. If I, therefore, the master and teacher, have washed your feet, you ought to wash one another's feet. I have given you a model to follow, so that as I have done for you, you should also do. (John 13:14-15)

The "Last Supper Discourse" follows the washing of the feet. This is when Jesus emphasizes the call to *love one another as I have loved you* (John 13:34). Jesus tells us to live in his love and our joy will be complete (John 15:10-11).

Through the precious gift of the Eucharist, Jesus is transforming us into himself: living, serving, and loving as he did. However, remember that Jesus is the Good Shepherd, not a micro-manager (see Chapter 20). God won't do this without us. We are invited to participate in the transforming power of God's grace. It doesn't happen *to* us. It happens *with* us. We need to be receptive to cooperating with the gift of grace.

~~~~~

*JoAnn recalls when her husband of 25 years announced his decision to leave her and their four children. "I hadn't told many people; I just didn't know how to talk about it. My teenage son had a game and needed me to bring him something for dinner, so I stopped at a deli. A neighbor who had boys the same age as mine sees me and—just being friendly—casually asks how things are going. I started to cry, sobbing and wailing uncontrollably to the point that she had to escort me outside. I can't tell you why I lost it with her. But when I went back to my son's game, I was somehow able to cope. To me, the Eucharist is like the Sacred Heart of Jesus; you know how he holds it in his hand? With the Eucharist, you are able to hold someone else's heart in your hands for a while... holding their pain. People who don't have Christ can't do that."*

~~~~~

*Dan was working at Lowe's when a man walked in and started asking questions about pouring concrete. "When I went to ask him for more information, the guy just stops, looks at me, and says that he just lost his wife. I start telling him how years ago, I lost my wife... two strangers in the middle of Lowe's. I ended up carrying this man's burden for a while. I didn't even know him. That is Eucharist."*

~~~~~

In the *Catechism for Adults*, when the U.S. Catholic Bishops discuss how the Eucharist has the power to transform us, they stress our receptivity. One way to do this is to pray: "Lord, take me. Bless me. Break me. Make me a part of your saving, sacrificial gift for the world's bodily and spiritual needs."[32]

Such a powerful transformation takes time. After all, Christ is transforming us into himself, not the other way around.

3. How have you experienced or witnessed the transforming power of the Eucharist?

4. What insight in this chapter speaks to you most at this time? Why?

5. What will you do to be more receptive to participating in the transforming power of Christ?

---

[32] United States Conference of Catholic Bishops (USCCB) (2012-04-02). *United States Catholic Catechism for Adults* (Kindle Locations 3380-3383). Kindle Edition.

# Chapter 22

# Service and Justice

*Years ago, I took a group of high school students to work at an orphanage in Mexico. In addition to showering the children with attention and affection, we did a bunch of home-improvement style projects – from cleaning to painting to repairs. The poverty was staggering. While we helped both physically and financially, it was abundantly clear that our charity was not going to bring about a real and lasting change.*

*That evening, we did the Mission-Trip-Circle-Up conversation to discuss and process our day. One student, Travis, was extremely conflicted: "I feel really good about myself, but I feel guilty for feeling that way. We have so much, and they have so little. It just doesn't make any sense; I don't like the fact that I feel so good about myself."*

~~~~~

It's common to hear people say that they "feel good" when they do service. After all, it feels good to do a good deed. It is important that we don't dismiss this as selfish or some sort of mistaken sense of "superiority" because from the Christian perspective, this goes a whole lot deeper.

Doing service on behalf of justice feels good because when we do it, we participate in true *agapic* love. Jesus called us to love one another as he loved us, to participate in *agape* (John 13:34, 15:12). This was not a "to-do-list" task, but an invitation. The act of selfless giving in service (and in love) feels great because in it, we experience the divine.

1. Tell of a time when you volunteered to do service and were filled with that "feel-good" feeling.

The call to service and justice is deeply rooted in Scripture and Tradition, yet Catholic Social Teaching is commonly referred to as "our best kept secret" because most people don't realize that there is even a connection between faith and justice.[33]

## Old Testament

The call to justice permeates the Old Testament. As the Jewish people would learn to become a people of God, they would learn that God is a "God of justice" (Is 30:18), and God's justice is concerned with giving preference to the poor (Ps 140:12). The Hebrew word most often used for "poor" in the Old Testament is *anawim* [AH-NA-WEEM], which refers to orphans, widows, and foreigners. In that culture, these three groups were without an income-producing tie to the land and were therefore, unable to provide for themselves. Without the assistance of the community, the *anawim* would go hungry and die.[34]

The prophets continually call for the people of Israel to care for the poor. Both Isaiah and Micah criticize people who go through the ritual motions of worship while failing to care for the poor (see Isaiah 58:1-8 and Micah 6:1-8). Micah explicitly tells the people of Israel that what God wants is simply for us to act with justice, love with kindness, and walk humbly with God (Micah 6:8).

2. What stands out for you regarding the call to justice in the Old Testament? Explain why.

---

[33] This expression is widely used among theorists that write about Catholic Social Teaching. Most explicitly, the phrase was used in an excellent resource by Peter J. Henriot, Edward P. DeBerri, and Michael J. Schultheis, entitled *Catholic Social Teaching: Our Best Kept Secret* (Center of Concern, Washington D.C., 2001, org. 1985).

[34] The Scripture references I will use in this chapter come from my book *Living the Vision: A Pastoral Guide to Service Learning in Catholic High Schools* (Lulu, 2008). As indicated in its title, I wrote this book as a professional resource, to assist high schools in forming service learning programs that are connected with the call to justice in Scripture and Tradition. In Chapter 2, I give a detailed explanation of the theological foundation for the call to justice.

## New Testament

The call to justice continues in the New Testament. Early in his ministry, when Jesus goes into the synagogue to read, he intentionally chose to proclaim specific words from Isaiah that draw attention to liberating the poor and oppressed:[35]

> The Spirit of the Lord is upon me, because he has anointed me to bring glad tidings to the poor. He has sent me to proclaim liberty to captives and recovery of sight to the blind, to let the oppressed go free, and to proclaim a year acceptable to the Lord. (Luke 4:18-19)

In the "Greatest Commandment" (Matthew 22:34-40) we are reminded to love God and neighbor.[36] In the Parable of the Good Samaritan (Luke 10:29-37), Jesus takes the time to explain that "being a neighbor" means to care for people in need. Who is my neighbor? Anyone in need. In Matthew 25, Jesus takes this a step further, connecting justice with our salvation.

> "For I was hungry and you gave me food, I was thirsty and you gave me drink, a stranger and you welcomed me, naked and you clothed me, ill and you cared for me, in prison and you visited me." Then the righteous will answer him and say, "Lord, when did we see you hungry and feed you, or thirsty and give you drink? When did we see you a stranger and welcome you, or naked and clothe you? When did we see you ill or in prison, and visit you?" And the king will say to them in reply, "Amen, I say to you, whatever you did for one of these least brothers of mine, you did for me." (Matthew 25:35-40)

Lest we forget, the Letter of James reminds believers of the importance of Jesus message: faith without works is dead (James 2:17).

3.  What stands out for you regarding the call to justice in the New Testament? Explain why.

---

[35] Luke 4:17 says that when Jesus was handed the scroll from Isaiah, he "found the passage where it was written." There was not a "reading of the day" as Catholics are accustomed to in the Lectionary. Jesus searched for and found the passages from Isaiah 61:1-2 and 58:6, wove them together, and intentionally proclaimed them.

[36] In *Living the Vision*, when I discuss the "Greatest Commandment," I explained that "Jesus' words are in continuity with Jewish tradition (Dt 6:4-5; Lv 19:18) and summarize the whole of the Decalogue (Ex 20:1-17). The essence of Christian teaching is this dual message of love, wherein we love God *by* loving our neighbor."

## Catholic Social Teaching

While the call to justice has always been part of the Christian tradition, it has really been in the past 125 years that the Church has given a great deal of attention to identifying "principles" of Catholic Social Teaching and encouraging the faithful to apply them to their cultural context.[37]

To this end, the World Synod of Bishops was commissioned by Pope Paul VI in 1965 to help the Church attend to "the signs of the times"[38] and respond to the needs of the world. In 1971, the World Synod of Bishops wrote *Justitia in Mundo* (Justice in the World), and definitively declared that working for justice is key to our faith.

> Action on behalf of justice and participation in the transformation of the world fully appear to us as a constitutive dimension of the preaching of the Gospel, or in other words, of the Church's mission for the redemption of the human race and its liberation from every oppressive situation (*JM* 6).

In 1998, the U.S. Catholic Bishops wrote *Sharing Catholic Social Teaching: Challenges and Directions* with the intention of helping the Catholic faithful by identifying the seven key themes of social justice that can be found in the heritage of Church documents.

**"Respect for Human Dignity"** must be present from the moment of natural conception to the moment of natural death, and everything in-between.

The **"Call to Family, Community, and Participation"** respects the social nature of humankind. We must support (not undermine) the family as a central, social institution. We must also support the right and duty of every person to participate in their community.

The **"Rights and Responsibilities"** of each human person must be respected, protected, and fulfilled. Each person has a fundamental right to life and basic human needs. Moreover, we each have a responsibility to ensure the rights of each person is respected. Both personal responsibility *and* social responsibility are needed.

The **"Option for the Poor and Vulnerable"** takes the message of the "least of my brothers and sisters" from Matthew 25:40, and understands that as economic, social, and political decisions are made, we must put the needs of the poor and vulnerable first.

---

[37] In *Living the Vision*, when I introduce Catholic Social Teaching, I offer a more detailed explanation of why the Church hasn't always focused on the call to justice: "With all that Jesus' holistic vision for the fullness of life in the world held, the message of the Reign of God was not the central concern of the apostles in the 1st Century. After Jesus' death and resurrection, establishing the Church to proclaim Jesus as the Christ became the focus of the disciples. Although charity and works of mercy were always part of the Christian tradition, until the late 19th Century, emphasis continued to be placed on establishing the church, not establishing the Reign of God....[W]hat happened in the late 19th Century? In 1891, Pope Leo XIII wrote *Rerum Novarum*, 'The Condition of Labor.' This document was the first of its kind, and set the stage, so to say, for what is referred to as Catholic Social Teaching. In the hundred (plus) years which would follow *Rerum Novarum*, the papacy and bishops would follow Leo XIII's example of applying Christian principles of human dignity and the common good to the circumstances of the day."

[38] The expression "signs of the times" comes from the Second Vatican document *Gaudium et Spec* (4).

**"The Dignity of Work and the Rights of Workers"** is the principle that insists that human people always take prescience over profits. "The economy must serve the people, not the other way around. Work is more than a way to make a living; it is a form of continuing participation in God's creation" (*SCST*).

**"Solidarity"** is the principle that points to the inter-connectedness of all human persons; we are one human family. We *are* our brothers' and sisters' keepers. "Learning to practice the virtue of solidarity means learning that 'loving our neighbor' has global dimensions in an interdependent world" (*SCST*).

**"Care for God's Creation"** recognizes that our earth is God's creation. Humankind has the God-given responsibility to be good stewards of the earth. We show respect for our Creator by how well we care for His creation. "This environmental challenge has fundamental moral and ethical dimensions that cannot be ignored" (*SCST*).

It is important that we hear the call of Catholic Social Teaching to be one of "faithful citizenship." Therein, the Church does not endorse one particular party. Rather, it challenges both parties to practice social justice.

4.  Which aspect of Catholic Social Teaching stands out for you? In what ways do you feel affirmed? Where do you feel challenged? Explain why.

The key to living out the call to justice is to see that every time we serve *the least* of our brothers and sisters, we are serving God. We must do what we can with what we have been given.

~~~~~

*Laurie was volunteering in the food pantry for SafePlace, an organization that provides safety and healing for people and families that have experienced domestic violence and/or sexual assault, helping the residents "shop" for their families for the week. There was a little boy who accompanied his mother in line. When they asked for cereal, and he saw the one and only option was a tasteless, full-of-fiber bran, he started to cry to his mother, "I don't want that kind. I want our regular kind. Why do we have to be here? I just want to go back with Dad." The emotional devastation of every woman in the room could be felt.*

*"It's the littlest things that we take for granted that can bring such simple joy for those who are so broken and vulnerable," Laurie remarked. Later that night, she posted a simple request to her local friends on Facebook. In addition to cereal and pancake mix*

*for kids, the Moms wanted popcorn and chips for movie night, and as an extra special treat, some boxed cake or cookie mixes.*

~~~~~

Laurie's simple, specific post helped direct the "givers" generosity to meet the "recipients" needs and wants. But she also did a tremendous service to raising awareness of the social issues surrounding domestic violence, as well as offering both a model and vehicle of charity to her 300+ Facebook friends, some of whom might never have considered the multitude of difficulties a victim of domestic violence faces.

~~~~~

*When Laurie told her mother this story, she was not surprised by her mother's generous offer to finance a "treats" run to stock the pantry. But in reflection, Laurie asked an important question: "It's great that my Mom is buying them groceries this month, but what about next month?"*

~~~~~

Laurie's question points to the difference between "charity" that temporarily alleviates the burden of a crisis and true "justice" that brings about lasting change. Catholic Social Teaching affirms that both are needed. Justice should always be what we are ultimately working towards, but charity is essential in the meantime. In charity, we find endless ways to help those in need.

> There are different kinds of spiritual gifts but the same Spirit; there are different forms of service but the same Lord; there are different workings but the same God who produces all of them in everyone. (1 Corinthians 12:4-6)

As an organization, SafePlace is committed to educating the community to break the cycle of violence, but they rely upon volunteers in the meantime to help families in crisis. Everything that Laurie was doing for SafePlace is important – from personally volunteering to raising awareness by telling stories to posting donation requests on Facebook. But she's not in the financial position to stock the pantry. That's ok. There are many parts. We are all one body. Without the time to shop or undergo training for volunteering, her mother donated money. That's all she was in the position to do at the moment. That's ok. There are many parts. We are all one body.

When it comes to doing service—when it comes to a faith that does justice—we need to avoid the two unhelpful extremes: on the one hand, don't be tempted to think that *it all depends on you* to do everything. That's what we call a Messiah complex. And honestly, we already have one of those. Secondly, don't think there is only one way to help. Do what you can. Where you can. When you can. There are many parts. We are all one body.

5. In what ways are you currently working for justice or helping those in need with charity?

6. The call to justice is all-encompassing, covering many areas of life. Is there a new commitment that you feel called to make? What steps will you take?

# Chapter 23

# Truth and Lies

⟁

You shall not bear false witness against your neighbor. (Exodus 20:16)

The Eighth Commandment calls us to respect truth. God is the God of Truth. Jesus tells us "I am the way and the truth and the life" (John 14:6). Respect for truth and honesty are the foundation of good relationships, which means that we must both *be truthful* and be honest in *seeking* the truth. We must share the truth with love and kindness, while respecting the privacy and dignity of all involved.

For a variety of different reasons, each of us has our own struggle with truthfulness.

~~~~~

*Ashley recalls a story from her youth. "I was in 5ᵗʰ grade, and I was forging my mom's name to my papers. It all started out because I simply forgot to get one paper signed and didn't want to get into trouble, but then I just kept on doing it for all the papers – good and bad. At a Parent-Teacher conference, my mom saw one of the papers, found out, and confronted me. And that's when the one lie led to an elaborate web of cover-up lies. First, I told my mom she did sign it; she just forgot. But my mom was smarter than that and didn't believe me. Part of my punishment was to go in and tell my teachers what I had done. Instead of telling them, I continued to lie. I came home and told my mom everything she would want to hear: that my teacher was very upset and disappointed, but glad I learned the lesson and would never do that again. She believed me, and I thought that was the end of it. Then my mom ran into Mrs. Opfer, one of my teachers, while she was out walking in her neighborhood. When my mom started talking about the forgery and accountability, Mrs. Opfer had no idea what she was talking about. The next day, when I saw her at school, Mrs. Opfer told me how disappointed and hurt she was. I had destroyed her trust – not by the first lie, but the series of lies after that. I'll never forget what she said, 'Trust is like a tree; when you chop it down it takes a long time to grow back.' All these years later, and I still feel ashamed about what I did. I never forgot that lesson. To this day, trust is one of the most important things for me in every one of my relationships."*

~~~~~

1. What is your own attitude towards truth and lies? Why do you feel that way? Who or what influenced you?

## What exactly do we mean by "a lie"?

The *Catechism* uses the words of St. Augustine: "A *lie* consists in speaking a falsehood with the intention of deceiving" (CCC, 2482). There are big lies and small, "white lies," and, certainly the *"gravity of a lie* is measured against the nature of the truth it deforms" (CCC, 2484). Though the intent of the lie and the circumstances surrounding it are taken into consideration, it is wrong to speak a falsehood of any level because lies—big and small—erode the foundational trust in a relationship.

It's easy for us to see the evil of big lies. Giving a false witness under oath (perjury) compromises justice. Adultery and theft each involve lies and violate commandments in their own right.

For the smaller lies, however, we tend to rationalize away our responsibility to uphold the truth. Honoring the Eighth Commandment requires quite a bit of the virtue of fortitude (or courage) along with the virtue of prudence (or wisdom).

## Gossip

Most of us—men and women, alike—struggle with gossip to some degree. Many of us want to classify gossip as simply spreading lies, but it is more about abusing, manipulating, and disrespecting truth. Gossip actually has three levels, which Tradition calls calumny, detraction, and rash judgment (see CCC, 2477). Calumny is what most think of when they hear the word gossip: spreading false rumors with the intent to damage another's reputation. This is obviously wrong, yet people try to rationalize by demonizing the victim as deserving such harsh treatment. Christians are called to love our enemies and pray for those who persecute us (Matthew 5:44). Revenge is never morally permissible.

Rash judgment is the kind of gossip that quite simply involves being judgmental. This happens when we are on the receiving end of second-hand information, which we use to we pass judgment on the character of someone. *I heard "x" about "y."* When we assume third party information is true, and find fault with the moral character of others, we are guilty of gossip. Rash judgment violates the Eighth Commandment because it dishonors the source of truth, damages the person's reputation, and erodes trust.

Detraction involves disclosing private information about someone without good reason. We do this when we complain and vent about another's faults and failings to a third party – particularly when we disclose details, knowing that we are not asking for advice on how to solve a problem. How often have we discussed someone else's personal life without their knowledge? How often have we been "nosey," seeking details about things that are none of our business? Private information should not be divulged without good reason (CCC, 2491). Sometimes this is even done under the guise of prayer. Like rash judgment, detraction damages a person's reputation and destroys trust.

Avoiding gossip is difficult when we engage in conversation with others who regularly "talk about others," whether in judgment or detraction. It takes fortitude and prudence to respond with firm, but loving kindness. Whether we end the discussion with a polite, "*I don't feel comfortable talking about this,*" or we insist on directly involving the person in question, respecting the Eighth Commandment means refusing to participate in gossip.

> 2. In what way have you struggled with gossip? Recall the "roles people play" from Chapter 12: perpetrator, bystander, target, and ally. When it comes to each form of gossip, what role have you played?

**Lovingly Honest Communication**

Another area of truth-telling that people struggle with is being "lovingly honest." Sometimes we focus on "love" at the expense of "truth," and rationalize lying because we don't want to hurt feelings. Or we may rationalize that we're doing the person a favor by "protecting" them from the truth. In some cases, we may even rationalize that it's easier to lie than deal with the ramifications of telling the truth. What we don't consider is the negative impact dishonesty has: it damages a person's relationship with the truth (CCC, 2483), it undermines trust among people, and "it tears apart the fabric of social relationships" (CCC, 2486).

Truth and honesty are the foundation of relationships. We have the right to expect truthful communication, and we have the responsibility to respond with loving honesty. Likewise, we need to get in the habit of expecting truthful responses to the questions we ask. If we don't want (or can't handle) the truth, then we are part of the problem.

While some struggle with being honest in their communication, others have no problem with speaking the truth. Here, we focus on "truth" at the expense of "love" and struggle with communicating honesty with kindness and tact. Being "blunt" is a mixture of a lack of love, as well as a lack of prudence for how, when, where, and *if* to deliver a message of truth.

It is worth pausing to consider *if* one should deliver a message of truth. We do not have an unconditional right to information; some things are private or not your news to share. The Eighth Commandment does not give us blind permission to dispense truth. "This requires us in concrete situations to judge whether or not it is appropriate to reveal the truth to someone who asks for it." (CCC, 2488)

3. How well do you practice (or how much do you struggle with) lovingly honest communication? Do you have a harder time being truthful or being loving?

4. Who do you know that manages to practice this with grace? How can you learn from their example?

## Truthful Actions and Words

We honor the truth when we witness to it in both our actions and words. This is especially the case with our faith.

> The duty of Christians to take part in the life of the Church impels them to act as witnesses of the Gospel and of the obligations that flow from it. This witness is a transmission of the faith in words and deeds. Witness is an act of justice that establishes the truth or makes it known. (CCC, 2472)

One area some of us struggle with is *exaggerating*. We may rationalize that we do not intend harm when we manipulate the details of a truthful situation, rather we insist that it makes for a better story! However, when we exaggerate, we are undermining our credibility and diminishing others' trust in our word.

Hypocrisy – saying one thing and doing another – discredits the witness of faith. Honoring the Eighth Commandment doesn't demand unreasonable perfection so much it compels us to aim for integrity while practicing humility. For this reason, boasting and bragging are offenses against the truth. So is sarcasm, particularly "when it is aimed at disparaging someone by maliciously caricaturing some aspect of [their] behavior" (CCC, 2481). When we come to expect hypocrisy, boasting, bragging, or sarcasm from someone, once again, it undermines their credibility and diminishes our trust.

Some of us have the remarkable gift of persuasion (or we know someone who does). When we seek to convince others, we must be careful to do so while honoring the Eighth Commandment. While affirmation speaks the truth about another's goodness, flattery distorts that truth with inappropriate praise. We cross the line to adulation when the praise becomes excessive, particularly if we have a malicious intent. These behaviors are manipulative; they distort the truth with the intent of using people. When a person uses these sorts of practices to achieve a self-serving end, they do more harm than the initial interaction. They damage the trust upon which relationships are built.

5. How well do you practice (or how much do you struggle with) truthful actions and words? Have you been hurt by any of these negative behaviors in others? Have you ever hurt others by abusing trust or distorting the truth?

6. Are there other areas of "respect for truth" that need attention? Explain.

7. Name three things you will work on to better honor the Eighth Commandment. What is your plan of action?

# Chapter 24

# Even Jesus Needed Downtime

◣

*My childhood home was a 1000 square foot raised ranch; five people, one bathroom. My mom's favorite form of relaxation has always been taking nice, long, hot baths. Thus, it was not unusual for my siblings and I to unabashedly enter the bathroom as needed while Mom was soaking in the tub. I mean, isn't that what the shower curtain is for? The thing is that we didn't necessarily enter to use the facilities. At any point in Mom's bath, there may be one, two, or all three of us just talking with her: laying on the floor, sitting on the hamper, or lounging on the (closed-lidded) toilet seat with feet propped on the side of the tub as if in a Lazy Boy… just talking. One day in my adolescence, Mom kind of got a little frustrated with the audience situation. "Why do you all follow me in here when I take a bath?!" Speaking from the heart, I responded, "Because it's the one time we can talk to you without you going anywhere." Mom was a little taken aback, thought for a bit, and simply said, "Oh…"*

~~~~~

From childhood through young adulthood, whenever I thought of this story, I recalled the honest yearning in my heart to have uninterrupted quality time with my Mom. Now, as a mother myself, my whole understanding of this family story changed. I cringe at my Mom's lack of personal, private downtime. In fact, now, when I read the story of Jesus healing the paralytic in Mark, I hear something that I never noticed before becoming a mother.

> When Jesus returned to Capernaum after some days, it became known that he was at home. Many gathered together so that there was no longer room for them, not even around the door, and he preached the word to them. They came bringing to him a paralytic carried by four men. Unable to get near Jesus because of the crowd, they opened up the roof above him. After they had broken through, they let down the mat on which the paralytic was lying. When Jesus saw their faith, he said to the paralytic, "Child, your sins are forgiven." (Mark 2:1-5)

As a mother, I read this thinking – oh my, poor Jesus! Not a moment to himself! There was no room in the house so they opened the roof above him?

Mark, the shortest, most action-packed Gospel is the quickest, easiest read. Go back to just before this scene into Chapter 1. After Jesus finished his 40 days in the desert, he begins his ministry, calls his disciples and started teaching. "His fame spread everywhere throughout the whole region of Galilee" (Mark 1:28). Then Mark's Gospel explains that Jesus leaves the synagogue and goes to the house of Simon-Peter, cures his mother-in-law of sickness, and word spread. The next thing he knew, "The whole town was gathered at the door" (Mark 1:33). The *whole town*? At this point, part of me is wondering what my Mom was complaining about with just three of us in the bathroom.

Jesus gets up very early the next morning before dawn, and goes off to a deserted place to pray (Mark 1:35), because he knew that this was his *only chance* to be alone, refresh, recharge, and reconnect with God through prayer. Still, "those that were with him pursued him" (Mark 1:36).

The poor guy was giving everyone everything he has to give, selflessly, completely, without hesitation… and he can't catch a break. He wakes up early to recharge with some quiet prayer time, and those that were with him *pursued* him.

Upon finding him, his disciple Simon-Peter tells him "Everyone is looking for you" (Mark 1:37).

So not only are his plans for a moment of peace thwarted, but those closest to Jesus are actually giving him a guilt trip for not being *more* available.

1.  Can you relate to Jesus? Have you ever felt pursued? Explain.

As a person who gives her time, energy, and effort to others, I can relate to Jesus in this situation. I can relate to the frustration of thwarted plans for alone time, but I can also learn from Jesus' example.

No matter how many times his plans were thwarted, Jesus pursued time alone to pray. Even Jesus needed downtime to quietly reflect, refresh, and recharge. Those precious times alone with God gave him the strength, courage, and wisdom to be fully present and available to the children of God. Because, as he told Simon-Peter, "For this purpose have I come" (Mark 1:38). Jesus knew how important downtime—time to pray—was to being able to fulfill his purpose. In this, Jesus was showing us how we all need to practice the Third Commandment.

The Third Commandment calls us to keep holy the Sabbath, which is to be a day dedicated to renewing our covenant with God.

> Remember the Sabbath day, to keep it holy. Six days you shall labor, and do all your work; but the seventh day is a Sabbath to the Lord your God; in it you shall not do any work. (Exodus 20:8-10; Deuteronomy 5:12-15)

We know that the Third Commandment calls us to set aside time to worship God in community (i.e., go to Mass), but what we often miss is the *theological concept of Sabbath*. Certainly, we are called to participate in the Sunday Eucharist, but we are also called to rest and be refreshed.

> God's action is the model for human action. If God "rested and was refreshed" on the seventh day, [humankind] too ought to "rest" and should let others, especially the poor, "be refreshed." (CCC, 2172)

Sabbath recalls the six days of God's work in Creation. The U.S. Catholic Bishops put it perfectly: "God's 'rest' on the seventh day was his contemplative gaze enjoying the good of creation, especially its crown in man and woman. It was not a matter of divine inactivity, but rather the deeper 'work' of contemplation and the restful act of loving us."[39] On our day of rest, we are to engage in recreation and leisure that helps us re-create our inner life. Sabbath "is a time for reflection, silence, cultivation of the mind, and meditation which furthers the growth of the Christian interior life" (CCC, 2186).

Ideally, the theological concept of Sabbath occurs on Sunday, in accordance with keeping holy the Lord's Day. "Traditional activities (sport, restaurants, etc.), and social necessities (public services, etc.), require some people to work on Sundays, but everyone should still take care to set aside sufficient time for leisure" (CCC, 2187). Even if it cannot be on Sunday, we must make rest and re-creation a priority in our lives.

Sabbath is about stopping, not doing…just being. Sabbath is about refreshing the soul and re-creating our passion and joy through recreation. It is reconnecting with our best selves and the God who created us. The *theological concept* of Sabbath is not limited to a day of the week. Moments of Sabbath are available to us all week long. We can seek Sabbath moments in formal experiences of prayer, Adoration, or daily Eucharist, or we open ourselves to seeking other refreshing practices, activities, and awareness.

~ ~ ~ ~ ~

---

[39] United States Conference of Catholic Bishops (USCCB) (2012-04-02). *United States Catholic Catechism for Adults* (Kindle Locations 5279-5281). United States Conference of Catholic Bishops (USCCB). Kindle Edition.

*Hannah finds Sabbath moments in nature. "I have always loved the beach, especially the way the view just seems to go on forever. The vast openness of the horizon reminds me of the expansive, unending love of God. And in that moment, I am with God. There are some days that I notice this same expansive beauty in the big, blue sky of Texas. The other day while driving, I almost needed to pull over because I was so taken by the beauty. The clouds were in perfect rows, like He had just placed them there as a reminder of His perfection and unending love for me. Every time the vast openness and expansiveness of nature catches my breath, I'm reminded of the unconditional and beautiful love God has for me. It leaves me feeling peaceful and reminds me to be still and rest in Him. Receiving and looking upon the Eucharist reminds me of the same thing." When Hannah is open to these moments of grace, she is filled with an awareness of the Divine.*

~~~~~

Hobbies provide tremendous opportunity for Sabbath moments: gardening, painting, crafting, woodworking, journaling, reading, running, etc. Personal practices such as taking a long, hot bath, reclining in the hammock, rocking in a favorite chair, enjoying a special view, or finding a way to savor every sip of your favorite morning beverage can likewise provide Sabbath moments. Sabbath moments are also available to us in those quality-time conversations when we connect with friends or when we play together as a family – at the pool, on vacation, at home playing a game, or simply around the dinner table laughing. It's not the activity itself that is virtuous, it is the experience of reconnecting with your innermost-self and God.

2. What do you do with your rest time? Which leisure activities refresh your soul? Where do you seek (and find) Sabbath moments? How often do you actually seek Sabbath moments in your week?

In today's culture, busy-ness is valued. Over-scheduling is valued. Obligations take precedence over spiritual leisure.[40] Rest, relaxation, and re-creation are not valued. Whether downtime is dismissed as laziness or considered a luxury, often it is not something we are encouraged to regularly integrate into our lives.

Many of us see the value in the spiritual leisure of Sabbath but struggle with the follow-through, in part because we feel that we don't have enough time to fit it "all" in. It is that very stance—*fitting it all in*—that is the problem. We get to the point where our schedules determine our priorities instead of our priorities determining our schedules.[41]

Every time we say "yes" to one thing, we say "no" to something else. There comes a point where the more we say "yes" to our jobs, communities, kids' activities, schools, friends, family etc., the more we say "no" to the precious downtime of spiritual leisure. We don't just see this in ourselves; we also see it in our over-scheduled children.

At the same time, it is worth noting that true Sabbath involves spiritual leisure that refreshes the soul; recreation that re-creates. This is not the same as "time-wasters" like mindless internet surfing or binge television watching (nor does actual sleep count as spiritual leisure).

3. What are your biggest challenges when it comes to practicing the spiritual leisure of Sabbath?

---

[40] Donna Schaper often uses the phrase "spiritual leisure" in *Sabbath Sense: A Spiritual Antidote for the Overworked* (Augsburg Books, 1997) to indicate the intentional pauses in our time that are dedicated to the rest and re-creation in Sabbath.

[41] Stephen Covey addresses this dynamic in *Seven Habits for Highly Effective People* (Free Press, 1989). Covey's approach to being an "effective person" easily lends itself to value-centered Christian living, but it is up to the reader to define which values he or she wants to live out. In Habit 1, readers understand that we must do more than take responsibility for our decisions (and the consequences that follow); being *proactive* means we anticipate problems and plan accordingly. Then, in Habit 2, "Begin with the End in Mind," readers are challenged to explicitly express the vision they have for themselves. Here, we need to go beyond generalizations like "be a good Christian," and identify the actual values we want to practice. In Habit 3, readers are then instructed to "Put First Things First" by taking a closer look at whether or not our time management decisions match the mission and vision we expressed in Habit 2. Habit 3's examination of actual prioritizing and decision making provides tremendous insight for how to live out a commitment to Sabbath and honoring the Third Commandment.

Sabbath is an invitation into a way of being. It is not intended to control or limit us, but to nourish us. Recall Jesus' words:

The Sabbath was made for man, not man for the Sabbath. (Mark 2:27)

As we take the time to be nourished by Sabbath moments (and worshiping with our parish community on Sunday) we can see the difference it makes. We are more open and receptive to love and life. We are more present to our families, children, friends, and loved ones.

So by their fruits you will know them. (Matthew 7:20)

Robert Wicks calls this *availability*.[42] When you're "too available," you are giving to everyone but yourself, and you end up sabotaging your own efforts. When you're completely tapped, or wiped out, you're no good to anyone. You need to take care of yourself because it will make you a better you. True availability to others, to God, and to oneself, reflects a life filled with spirituality nurtured with Sabbath moments.

If you're not willing to Keep the Sabbath as a holy gift to yourself, do it for those you love and serve.

4. What decision will you make for yourself with regards to your own observance of Keeping the Sabbath?

---

[42] Robert Wicks discusses this in *Availability: The Spiritual Gift of Helping Others*. (The Crossroad Publishing Company, 1986).

# Chapter 25

# Friendship

Philia is the love of friends.  Close friends share a generous, affectionate love that surpasses acquaintances… that surpasses utility (what you can do for me).  *Philia* is a love of friends that embodies warmth, appreciation, companionship; friendship is about mutual sharing.

~~~~~

*In a good friendship, April explains, "there is true reciprocity of love, support, and transparency, leaving you feeling safe and inspired."*

~~~~~

*Though time may pass, Julie adds, "you pick up like no time has lapsed – instant love, instant comfort in every communication."*

~~~~~

Friends know us through-and-through and love us all the more.  Their genuine care and concern for our well-being is as warm as their hugs, handshakes, and arm-pats. We delight in their presence.   We savor the moments of quality time, the great conversations, the honesty, the fun, and the laughing.  The laughing is the best.

Much of friendship is based on common interests, activities, and values.  As people grow and change, the reality is that friendships need to grow, change, and adjust alongside… or they need to fade, if only temporarily.  As Christians, it can be difficult to step away from a friendship; after all, we are called to love.  But when Jesus calls us to love, it is *agape*, not *philia*.  *Philia* love is an enriching experience which Jesus, himself even enjoyed.  Yet Jesus didn't share *philia* with everyone he encountered.  There is something special about those whom we call friends.

1. Who are your friends?  How do you express and experience *philia* love with them?  How do your friends enrich your life?

Friendship has lots of categories: good-friends, old-friends, Mom-friends/Dad-friends, family-friends, work-friends, Facebook Friends… and they're all good, at least they have the potential to be.

Let's take a closer look at "Facebook Friends." Facebook helps us reacquaint with old friends from different points in our lives, especially if you have moved around quite a bit. Some "friends" from Facebook are just in the social network, more akin to friendly acquaintances. Some offer a lot of "water-cooler-didja-hear-about" conversation. Facebook allows friends to know about what's going on in each other's lives. When someone shares joy, we can smile with them. When someone shares pain, we can gather them in our thoughts and prayers. And how about the birthday-love from Facebook friends? It's certainly a different version of friendship than our grandparents experienced, but it's community all the same. At least it has the potential to be.

2. How does social media (like Facebook) or electronic communication (like email, texts, etc.) help or hinder your friendships?

That's the question, isn't it. Is Facebook a community of friends for you, or is it a network of acquaintances who alternate between boasting/bragging and complaining? In fact, that's the question that undergirds all of our friendships. Whether it's online or in-person, are our friendships about community, with whom we have fun, who challenges us, comforts us, supports us, and cheers us on… or are our friendships about competition, comparisons, put-downs, and criticism that leave us deflated and questioning our worthiness?

These sorts of draining relationships are sometimes called "toxic friendships" or "frenemies" (a combination of "friend" and "enemy"). Of course we never consciously enter into toxic friendships. At first the person is charming and supportive… until you need something which requires the person to give of themselves. There are times, due to understandable circumstances, which we are all incapable of giving to a friend in need. The toxic friend, however, doesn't just deny your request; instead, they belittle, berate, and humiliate you for even making a request. The toxic friend turns your genuine need into your character flaw.

~~~~~

*Ingrid explains, "When someone is toxic, they assume that things you've done in good faith are actually malicious because most of their own motivations are—if not malicious—at a minimum, self-serving."*

~~~~~

*As Mary Beth describes, "After talking or being with them, you feel like you're hungover. A headache from everything you said being misunderstood or not accepted, a sick stomach from questioning how you can be a better friend, lethargic from putting your feelings out on the table only to be dismissed, and questioning whether or not to drink— talk to them—again."*

~~~~~

How is a Christian to respond to toxic friendships? First and foremost, we need to recognize that these are not experiences of *philia* love. As a matter of self-love and respect for human dignity, we may need to take a step back and remove ourselves from harm. Jesus calls to practice *agape* (willing of another's good) with everyone, not the closeness of *philia*. While we may not be able to open ourselves to the vulnerability of friendship with people who hurt us, we can still act with care and concern for their well-being.[43]

3. Have you had an experience with a toxic friendship (or frenemies)? How did you deal with the pain and disappointment? How did your response measure up to the call to respect your own human dignity? In what way were/are you able to practice *agape*?

The joy and love of true friendship is sustaining. Jesus shared *philia* love with his closest friends.

No one has greater [*agape*] than this, to lay down one's life for one's [*philia*]. You are my [*philia*] if you do what I command you. I no longer call you slaves, because a slave does not know what his master is doing. I have

---

[43] The passage from Scripture known as *pearls before swine* also speaks to the dynamic of toxic friendships. "Do not give what is holy to dogs, or throw your pearls before swine, lest they trample them underfoot, and turn and tear you to pieces" (Matthew 7:6).

called you [*philia*], because I have told you everything I have heard from my Father. (John 15:13-15)

Within the group of friends you *philia*, different people have different roles. Beyond the title of "best friend," there are certain people in our lives that are part of our "inner circle." These are the close friends you appoint to a place of honor in your life. Some call it their "Personal Board of Directors" or "The Brain Trust." These are the folks who we tend to check in with regarding our life decisions, and the ones with whom we cannot wait to share any "big" news. We may not always agree with the counsel offered by members of our Board, nor do we always follow their advice. However, we certainly listen to what they have to say – good or bad – because we value their input.

4.   Who have you appointed to your own Personal Board of Directors?

The friendships filled with *philia* love can touch us so deeply that they may even bring the Divine Presence into our lives. In *Touching the Holy*, Robert Wicks identifies four different kinds of friends that it is important to have in our lives.[44]

**The Prophet** is the friend who points out the truth and challenges us to take a closer look at how we are living our lives. Prophets prompt us to examine whether we are listening to God's voice and following our values or if we are being swayed by "other" voices. When the prophet-friend asks, "*What's that about?*" it makes us think. This is the friend who will speak the difficult truth (with love), despite discomfort or pain.

5.   Who are the Prophetic Friends in your life?

---

[44] In Robert Wicks book *Touching the Holy: Ordinariness, Self-Esteem and Friendship* (Ave Maria Press, 1992), he notes that it's certainly possible for one friend to have multiple roles; it is just important that each of the four roles are represented in our friendships. On the topic of friendships and their important impact on Christian discipleship, I also recommend *The Work of Your Life: Sustaining the Spirit to Teach, Lead, and Serve*, by Catherine Cronin Carotta (Harcourt 2003), which offers a summary of Wick's four friends, presenting them in the context of discerning one's calling.

**The Cheerleader** is that friend that offers unabashed, enthusiastic, unconditional acceptance. This is the person who helps us see the reflection of the loving face of God more readily in ourselves and others. When we've had a difficult day, this is the person we turn to for loving support and encouragement because they say just the right thing to nurture our own self-love. The cheerleader is the friend who offers the presence of God's mercy and love.

~~~~~

*My Grandpop was perhaps the greatest cheerleader there ever was. I'm proud to say that my Mom and my sister continue Grandpop's legacy of enthusiasm and acceptance. I can't wait to share news with them because they triple my own excitement. When I need affirmation, I call them. In their love and support, they remind me of God's goodness dwelling within me.*

~~~~~

6.   Who are the Cheerleader Friends in your own life?

**The Harasser** is the friend who helps keep us from taking ourselves too seriously. The harasser makes us laugh – especially at ourselves. Through friendship with the harasser, we avoid emotional burnout and/or unrealistic expectations of ourselves because they help us both regain and maintain perspective.

7.   Who are the Harasser Friends in your own life?

**The Spiritual Guide** helps us to identify our deepest fears, our soulful longings, and our treasured values. This is the person who helps us process experiences in our quest to make meaning of our lives. The spiritual guide prompts us to go deeper, not because of their own agenda, but because of who they are and how they love us. At different times in our lives, different people may have served in this role.

8.   Who are the Spiritual Guide Friends in your own life?

These four friends help to balance each other out. Too much cheerleader and not enough prophet might make a person a bit full of themselves... too much prophet and not enough cheerleader might make a person down on themselves... So we need all four kinds.

9. What insight are you coming to have for yourself on the topic of friends? Where do you feel affirmed? What needs to change?

# Chapter 26

# Hope

✦

1. Looking ahead, at the next few months (or years), what do you hope for?

2. If the question above (#1) had instead asked "what would you wish for," would your answer change at all?

Although we often use the words hope and wish interchangeably, there's a huge difference. Both are future oriented—for things we want to happen. When we wish for something we want to happen, we do so in a passive way: wanting something to happen to us without any effort on our part. (*I wish we would win the lottery.*) When we hope for something we want to happen, we actively participate in bringing it about. (*I hope my children grow up to be good, generous, loving people.*)

When we consider that hope is a theological virtue, what we're saying is that we are actively participating with God. The theological virtue of hope can be defined as trusting in the promises for the Kingdom of God and cooperating with God's grace to make the future happen.

Participating with God involves trust. As if to say, "*I trust that I am doing my best, taking personal, proactive responsibility. And I trust God is involved in the whole process, guiding my efforts and accomplishing things beyond my comprehension.*"

Pray as if everything depended on God and work as if everything depended on you. (CCC, 2834)[45]

Balancing the two – personal responsibility and trust in God – is a challenge. Most of us struggle with one of the two extremes:

Too Much God, Not Enough Me

–OR–

Too Much Me, Not Enough God

## Too Much God, Not Enough Me

Are you familiar with the contemporary parable about the man and the flood?

A man who lived by the river heard a radio report predicting severe flooding. Heavy rains were going to cause the river to rush up and flood the town, so all the residents were told to evacuate their homes. But the man said, "I'm religious. I pray. God loves me. God will save me." The waters rose up. A guy in a rowboat came along, and he shouted, "Hey, you in there. The town is flooding. Let me take you to safety." But the man shouted back, "I'm religious. I pray. God loves me. God will save me." A helicopter was hovering overhead, and a guy with a megaphone shouted, "Hey you, you down there. The town is flooding. Let me drop this ladder and I'll take you to safety." But the man shouted back that he was religious, that he prayed, that God loved him and that God will take him to safety. Well… the man drowned. And standing at the gates of St. Peter he demanded an audience with God. "Lord," he said, "I'm a religious man, I pray, I thought you loved me. Why did this happen?" God said, "I sent you a radio report, a helicopter and a guy in a rowboat. What are you doing here?"

When our reliance on God comes at the neglect of human action, we are not practicing the virtue of hope. Instead, we practice some wish-based "cheap-hope" where *God will provide* becomes equivalent to saying *God will do it all for me*. We are invited to participate in bringing about the Kingdom of God.

Sometimes, all we can do to help a situation is pray. And we should always pray. But when we can do something more–and it falls within our realm of responsibility–we should do so.

God created us in his image and likeness (Genesis 1:26-27), and bestowed upon us gifts and talents that he expects us to use (recall Chapter 9 "Called By God" and the

---

[45] The *Catechism* notes that this quote is attributed to St. Ignatius Loyola, cf. Joseph de Guibert, SJ, The Jesuits: Their Spiritual Doctrine and Practice, (Chicago: Loyola University Press, 1964), 148, n. 55.

Parable of the Talents, Matthew 25:14-30). We need to take these seriously as we practice the virtue of hope.

## Too Much Me, Not Enough God

On the other hand, there are those of us who take it to the other extreme: relying on human action alone and excluding God.

We recognize that the person in despair lacks hope. But too often this isn't an inability to practice the virtue of hope. Rather, despair–hopelessness–is a sign of a serious depression. Help is available for those who need it.

Who struggles with the practicing the virtue of hope?

- The Type-A who obsesses about every little detail
- The Control Freak who cannot let go
- The Worrier who is filled with anxiety
- The Complainer who loses perspective

When we think that everything is up to us, we are not practicing the virtue of hope. Here, the lack of hope involves the failure to trust God.

~~~~~

*When Maureen was asked to be the Spiritual Director for her parish's next Christ Renews His Parish (CRHP) retreat, she was overwhelmed. "I can't do this; I'm not qualified." The Continuation Committee recognized her gifts and talents, but Maureen was filled with anxiety. "This is an enormous responsibility. I cannot possibly lead and guide these women on their journey." In prayer and conversation with her loved ones, Maureen came to see that she was assuming that she alone was responsible for the direction of the retreat. Rather than envision her leadership as participating with God, she feared it was all up to her. Once she grounded herself in the virtue of hope, she was able to say yes. Throughout the process of formation, Maureen had to constantly remind herself that she was not in this alone. Rather, she was working with God: doing her best and trusting God to work in, with, and through her.*

~~~~~

Whether it's our parenting, our professional career, or our relationships, practicing the virtue of hope means that we are participating with God. Moreover, we are inviting God to participate with us in every nook and cranny of our lives.

Practicing the virtue of hope also means participating with others. We need to allow and encourage others to participate to the best of their abilities. That means putting down our "If you want it done right you have to do it yourself" banners. The social justice principle of subsidiarity means that we let each person do for themselves what they can. There is goodness in that. It's how Jesus did things, too.

It's important to note that our graced invitation to participate with God in hope was never intended to be a 50-50 proposition. It's not like we do our part and hand the rest off to God. Rather, there is value to our human efforts, but let us remember the First Commandment. God is still God. Like any virtue, practicing hope is something that we can get better at doing.

3. Where do you find success (and where do you struggle) in practicing the virtue of hope? Do you struggle more with "too much God" or "too much me"? Explain.

4. What is one thing you can do to improve your practice of the virtue of hope?

# Chapter 27

# Stewardship and Boundaries

✦

So much of our Christian faith is about loving one another and saying "Yes" to God.

As each one has received a gift, use it to serve one another as good stewards of God's varied grace. (1 Peter 4:10)

We are called to be good stewards. Stewardship is a way of understanding our role and relationship to God. In ancient times the metaphor of stewardship was clearly understood. God is the landowner and as his appointed stewards, our role was to be caretakers. The landowner would entrust the steward with the responsibility to care for the property, manage the affairs, make good use of the resources, and share those resources with others. The position of stewardship involves trust and accountability.[46]

~~~~~

*Although I have had plenty of good experiences of stewardship, one bad experience left a strong impression. Throughout my childhood, we would go on a family vacation each summer. My mom went to great lengths to leave the house perfectly clean so when we returned, it would be a welcome sight. One year my mom asked Lisa, a pre-teen neighbor to housesit: feed the cats, and water the plants. When we returned home, we discovered that she had made herself food, left a mess, and made long-distance phone calls. While it was far from "trashing the place," we—especially my mom—felt violated. We had trusted her to do this job… and instead she chose to take advantage of us.*

~~~~~

God has trusted us to do a job: care for creation. The way we practice discipleship is by being good stewards for God. This means we care for the earth and all of creation because we recognize that all of it (and all of us) belongs to God. As stewards, we are more than housesitters who do little more than wait for the homeowner to return.

---

[46] The U.S. Catholic Bishops *Pastoral Letter on Stewardship* (1992) explains "As Christian stewards, we receive God's gifts gratefully, cultivate them responsibly, share them lovingly in justice with others, and return them with increase to the Lord." United States Conference of Catholic Bishops, "To Be a Christian Steward: A Summary of the U.S. Bishops' Pastoral Letter on Stewardship" http://www.usccb.org/beliefs-and-teachings/what-we-believe/stewardship/index.cfm (Accessed June 20, 2014).

Stewards manage affairs and make good use of the gifts God has given, cultivate them, and share them with others. In practical terms, this involves our vocational calling in life and participating in the life of the Church. Stewardship is about how we actually live out saying "Yes" to God.

> 1. Stewards are caretakers, not owners. Stewardship recognizes the sovereignty of God as well as the important role we each have, cooperating with God. In what ways do you currently practice this stance in your own life? What areas of your life would benefit from a focus on this stance?

Some of us struggle with misappropriating the notion of Stewardship, particularly with regards to boundaries. On the one hand, there are those of us whose notion of stewardship is to "do all the things," take on too much, and burnout. On the other hand, there are those of us who end up getting too involved in lives of those we love and serve.

**Boundaries: Too Much "Yes"**

To a great extent, the struggle with taking on too much reflects a lack of the virtue of hope, as discussed in the last chapter. Not only does this lead to burnout, but when one takes on too much, they actually prevent others from the having ability to serve.

When we are tempted to think that "it's all up to us," what we're inadvertently doing is inserting ourselves as a "god." It's often called a "Messiah Complex" for that very reason. Those of us who struggle with taking on too much would benefit from reflecting on (and repeating) the wise words of John the Baptist, "I am not the Messiah" (John 1:20).[47] Likewise, the "Archbishop Oscar Romero Prayer: A Step Along the Way"

---

[47] At a liturgy in the Summer Session of the Institute of Religious Education and Pastoral Ministry (2001), Thomas Groome offered a reflection on John the Baptist which resonates deeply with people in ministry. Tom praises John's wisdom for knowing that he is not the Messiah. Tom invited the whole gathering of professional ministers at that liturgy to repeat those words aloud: "I am not the Messiah. I am not the Messiah. I am not the Messiah."

is a prayerful way for those of us who struggle with "taking on too much" to remember our role in stewardship.[48]

It helps, now and then, to step back and take a long view.

The kingdom is not only beyond our efforts, it is even beyond our vision.

We accomplish in our lifetime only a tiny fraction of the magnificent enterprise that is God's work.

Nothing we do is complete, which is a way of saying that the Kingdom always lies beyond us.

No statement says all that could be said.

No prayer fully expresses our faith.

No confession brings perfection.

No pastoral visit brings wholeness.

No program accomplishes the Church's mission.

No set of goals and objectives includes everything.

This is what we are about.

We plant the seeds that one day will grow.

We water seeds already planted, knowing that they hold future promise.

We lay foundations that will need further development.

We provide yeast that produces far beyond our capabilities.

We cannot do everything, and there is a sense of liberation in realizing that.

This enables us to do something, and to do it very well.

It may be incomplete, but it is a beginning, a step along the way, an opportunity for the Lord's grace to enter and do the rest.

We may never see the end results, but that is the difference between the master builder and the worker.

We are workers, not master builders; ministers, not messiahs.

We are prophets of a future not our own.

---

[48] Archbishop Oscar Romero (1917-1980) was an archbishop in El Salvador who spoke out against poverty and social injustice. He was assassinated *during* Mass by Salvadoran soldiers. As of June 2014, the Vatican is examining the possibility for Romero's canonization. Regarding the prayer, the U.S. Catholic Bishops note: "This prayer was composed by Bishop Ken Untener of Saginaw….As a reflection on the anniversary of the martyrdom of Bishop Romero, Bishop Untener included in a reflection book a passage titled 'The mystery of the Romero Prayer.' The mystery is that the words of the prayer are attributed to Oscar Romero, but they were never spoken by him." http://www.usccb.org/prayer-and-worship/prayers-and-devotions/prayers/archbishop_romero_prayer.cfm. (Accessed June 20, 2014).

2. Was there some aspect of "taking on too much" that resonated with you? Is there something in the Archbishop Oscar Romero prayer that spoke to you? Explain.

## Boundaries: Not Enough "No"

Sometimes, our "Yes" to God in stewardship gets misinterpreted as necessitating a "Yes" to everyone about every request for everything. Sometimes, in our efforts to help, we become overly invested in the life and growth of those that we are trying to love and serve. Other times, it is the people who we seek to serve that have difficulty respecting boundaries. Whether it is an inability to say "no" or hear (and respect) "no," a lack of boundaries is a problem.

In their book *Boundaries*, Dr. Henry Cloud and Dr. John Townsend break open Scripture to help readers understand that boundaries are not only important, but they are a gift from God.[49] Respecting boundaries helps each of us live out the call to stewardship – *with* one another, not *for* one another. One of the helpful insights that Cloud and Townsend offer comes by way of closely examining a passage from Galatians.

> Bear one another's burdens, and so you will fulfill the law of Christ. Each one must examine his own work, and then he will have reason to boast with regard to himself alone, and not with regard to someone else; for each will bear his own load. (Galatians 6:2, 4-5)

In Greek, the word "burdens" (*bear another's burdens*) conjures an image of an excessive amount of troubles that are so heavy, they weigh us down like boulders. However, the term "load" (*for each will bear his own load*) is closer to translating as every-day cargo, like a knapsack.[50] Of course, we are called to help others when they face excessive

---

[49] Henry Cloud and John Townsend. *Boundaries: When to Say Yes, How to Say No to Take Control of Your Life* (Zondervan, 1992).

[50] Cloud and Townsend examine this passage from Galatians several times throughout *Boundaries*, but on pages 30-31 they draw specific attention to the difference between being responsible "to" others and being responsible "for" others.

burdens. We are also expected to bear our own manageable, every-day load. If we try to take on another's every-day load, we are overstepping boundaries. If we try to thrust our every-day load upon others, we are overstepping boundaries.

Along these lines, there is a difference between being responsible *to* one another and being responsible *for* one another.[51] We *are* our brothers' and sisters' keepers (Genesis 4:9) in as much as we are responsible *to* care for one another. But as soon as we try to become responsible *for* one another's decisions, we actually take away their freedom. Our freedom to choose – to say yes or no – is essential to our humanity. It is because of our freedom that we have the ability to genuinely love and serve as stewards.

3. Can you relate to the distinction between "burdens" and "load"? Recall a time when you (or someone you know) had "burdens" and needed the help of others to manage. Contrast this with an experience of managing every-day-cargo.

4. What has been your experience with stewardship and respecting boundaries? Is this an area of success or struggle for you?

5. What are you coming to see for yourself when it comes to stewardship and boundaries? What can you do to improve your practice of true stewardship?

---

[51] Cloud and Townsend emphasize that "we are responsible to care about and help, *within certain limits*, others whom God places in our lives" (58).

# Chapter 28

# Longing

✦

There is a longing in the human heart – an indescribable sense of desire. The quest, the seeking, the yearning is a common experience that many authors write about. We see it in plays and movies, read it in books and poetry, hear and sing along with it in music. As we search and yearn, many of us can identify with the longing in Bono's voice in U2's song "I Still Haven't Found What I'm Looking For."[52]

~~~~~

*Dorothy was raised by her grandparents in a small town in Mexico. Both her grandparents and godparents had a positive impact on her formation and Catholic faith, but she recalls struggling, especially as a teenager with the sense of abandonment from her biological mother and father. Then at 13, she was traumatized by finding grandfather dead on the floor. Less than a year later, her beloved godfather contracted bacterial meningitis which led to a stroke, requiring a wheelchair and constant care. "This series of events depressed me, and I felt like I was in a state of nothingness, questioning the existence of God. For the longest time during my teenage years, I felt extremely lonely, unable to connect to anyone, and angry at the world."*

~~~~~

Sometimes this longing prompts philosophical questions about our existence: Why am I here? Who am I? What is the meaning of life? What is it all about? Where am I going? Why did this horrible thing happen? We look for answers. Sometimes this longing brings an awareness that something is missing. We may seek to fill it with material things, with monetary success, with high-powered, fast-paced lives, with experiences and adventures, with relationships… but we often find that nothing quite works. For some, the longing and awareness is overwhelming. It can bring depression and pain. Some choose to numb themselves to the sense of longing with alcohol or drugs… with addiction to a substance, to gambling, to sex, to pornography… But no matter where we look, no matter how we try, none of these people, places, or things bring a sense of fulfillment to our longing desire.

---

52 "I Still Haven't Found What I'm Looking For" is from U2's album *The Joshua Tree*, Island Records, 1987.

1. Can you relate to this sense of longing? Were there specific times in your life when you recalled the sense of desire? Explain.

There is an expression that is often used to describe the reason for this longing: we have a God-shaped hole in our hearts, which cannot be filled with anything other than God, no matter how hard we try.[53]

Find your delight in the Lord who will give you your heart's desire. (Psalm 37:4)

In his *Confessions*, St. Augustine tells how he struggled with misdirected longing and desire from his youth through his early 30's: parties, sex, and boasting… maneuvering himself into prestigious positions among the best and the brightest… hanging around with the wrong crowd… stealing just because… Augustine was raised Christian, but his intellectual pursuits led him down a multitude of other philosophical paths. It was during this time of his life that he prayed, "Lord make me chaste, but not yet!"[54]

Upon his conversion, Augustine found his longing and desire were fully and completely answered in God. He describes this understanding eloquently: "You have made us for yourself, and our heart is restless until it rests in you."[55]

The desire for God is written in the human heart, because we are created by God and for God; and God never stops drawing us into himself. Only in God will we find the truth and happiness we never stop searching for (CCC, 27). The Second Vatican Council noted this longing in *Gaudium et Spes* (The Church in the Modern World):

---

[53] The expression is attributed to French Mathematician, Blaise Pascal (1623-1662). The website www.ThinkExist.com offers the following as the original reference: "There is a God-shaped vacuum in the heart of every person, and it can never be filled by any created thing. It can only be filled by God, made known through Jesus Christ." http://thinkexist.com/quotation/there_is_a_god_shaped_vacuum_in_the_heart_of/166425.html. (Accessed June 22, 2014).

[54] This is a common shorthand version of the actual quote from *Confessions* Book 8, Chapter 7, Paragraph 17 "Grant me chastity and continence, but not yet."

[55] This quote is another common shorthand. The original passage reads: "for thou hast made us for thyself and restless is our heart until it comes to rest in thee," from *Confessions* Book 1, Chapter 1, Paragraph 1, and is also quoted in the *Catechism's* section on "The Desire for God," in CCC, 27.

Human dignity rests above all on the fact that humanity is called to communion with God. The invitation to converse with God is addressed to men and women as soon as they are born. For if people exist it is because God has created them through love, and through love continues to keep them in existence. They cannot live fully in the truth unless they freely acknowledge that love and entrust themselves to their creator. (*GS* 19)[56]

When we are able to connect our deep longing desire with the love and grace of God, we find fulfillment. Let us return to Dorothy's story:

~~~~~

*Four years later, at 17, Dorothy emigrated to the U.S. with her grandmother for her godfather's medical treatment. "I learned English, graduated from High School, went off to college, and after several bad relationships, I started seeking God. I sang with the church choir at college, and slowly I started to find some comfort in my heart." After graduating college and finding a job in aerospace research, Dorothy found herself coming out of another bad relationship, falling into depression, and questioning her existence. "I asked God to take me away. I wasn't happy at all, I always felt a deep emptiness in my heart. I also couldn't understand the concept of faith, especially with a job in science." In the midst of her questioning, Dorothy decided to go on a retreat. "The experience was so great! For the first time, I felt like God was talking to me... but actually, it was more of me being aware of His presence, and opening my heart and ears to listen to Him. In this moment of conversion, I was able to believe that God had me in the palm of His hands since I was born, and He has never abandoned me. I understood then that my mother was not at fault for leaving me, because I saw her action as an act of mercy and concern for my future. I had reached closure in a painful chapter in my life, and afterwards, I started loving myself and loving others."*

~~~~~

2.    Can you relate to St. Augustine's or Dorothy's story? Have you ever tried to fill that God-shaped hole in your heart with anything other than God?

---

[56] Austin Flannery, ed. *Vatican II: Constitutions, Decrees, Declarations.* Revised translation in inclusive language. (Northport: Costello Publishing, 1996). All quotes from the documents of Vatican II are from this edition. References are given in the text by paragraph number.

On St. Augustine's Feast Day in 2013, Pope Francis celebrated Mass with the Augustinian order of priests. In his homily, Pope Francis encouraged us to *be restless* in three areas of life: in our spiritual life, in our search for God, and in our love for others. Sometimes we can become complacent or stuck in a rut, particularly when it comes to our spiritual life. Pope Francis warns us against being "anesthetized" to restlessness. As a Christian, you must "look into your heart and ask yourself if you have a heart that wants great things or a heart that is asleep. Has your heart maintained that restlessness or has it been suffocated by things?"[57]

"Let yourself be restless for God." Pope Francis tells us. For it is that restlessness that keeps us *continuing the journey*.

3. How do you answer Pope Francis' question: "Has your heart maintained that restlessness or has it been suffocated by things?"

4. Take some time to flip back through the chapters in the book. Are there chapters or topics that you can feel that "restlessness" and would like to spend more time pursuing?

5. Make note of the next three things you will do to *Continue the Journey*.

---

[57] Catholic News Service. Aug-28-2013 "Pope says Christians Should Have Restless Hearts Like St. Augustine's" by Cindy Wooden http://www.catholicnews.com/data/stories/cns/1303694.htm. (Accessed June 23, 2014).

# Bibliography

American Catholic. "St. Anthony Messenger Ask the Wise Man: The Rift Between Jews and Samaritans." http://www.americancatholic.org/messenger/sep1996/wiseman.asp (accessed 31 May 2014).

Anti-Defamation League. "Roles People Play." 2003. http://archive.adl.org/education/holocaust/rolespeopleplayworksheet.pdf (accessed 31 May 2014).

Augustine. *Confessions*. Translated and edited by Albert C. Outler, 1955. http://www.ourladyswarriors.org/saints/augcon1.htm (accessed 26 June 2014).

Carotta, Catherine Cronin. *The Work of Your Life: Sustaining the Spirit to Teach, Lead, and Serve*. Orlando: Harcourt, 2003.

*Catechism of the Catholic Church*. Second Edition. Libreria Editrice Vaticana. Washington DC: United States Conference of Catholic Bishops. Kindle Edition, 2011.

Catholic Answers. "Who Were the Samaritans and Why Were They Important?" http://www.catholic.com/quickquestions/who-were-the-samaritans-and-why-were-they-important (accessed 31 May 2014).

Cloud, Henry and John Townsend. *Boundaries: When to Say Yes, How to Say No to Take Control of Your Life*. Grand Rapids: Zondervan, 1992.

Covey, Stephen R. *The Seven Habits of Highly Effective People: Powerful Lessons in Personal Change*. New York: Simon & Schuster, 1989.

Dienno-Demarest, Julie. *Living the Vision: A Pastoral Guide to Service Learning in Catholic High Schools*. Lulu, 2008.

Groome, Thomas H. *Educating for Life*. Allen: Thomas Moore, 1998

_____. *Sharing Faith*. Eugene: Wipf and Stock, 1998.

_____. *What Makes Us Catholic: Eight Gifts for Life*. San Francisco: Harper, 2002.

Henriot, Peter J., Edward P. DeBerri, and Michael J. Schultheis. *Catholic Social Teaching: Our Best Kept Secret*. Washington D.C.: Center for Concern, 2001.

Ignatian Spirituality. "Ignatian Prayer: The Daily Examen." http://www.ignatianspirituality.com/ignatian-prayer/the-examen/ (accessed 28 May 2014).

Jewish Virtual Library. "Concentration Camps: The Sonderkommando" by Jacqueline Shields. http://www.jewishvirtuallibrary.org/jsource/Holocaust/Sonderkommando.html (accessed 7 May 2014).

John Paul II. *Man and Woman He Created Them: Theology of the Body.* Translated by Michael Waldstein. Boston: Pauline Books, 2006.

_____. *Redemptoris Missio. On the Permanent Validity of the Church's Missionary Mandate.* 1990. http://www.vatican.va/holy_father/john_paul_ii/encyclicals/documents/hf_jp-ii_enc_07121990_redemptoris-missio_en.html (accessed 29 June 2014).

Lewis, C.S.. *The Great Divorce.* New York: Macmillan Publishing Company, 1946.

May, Gerald G. *The Dark Night of the Soul: A Psychiatrist Explores the Connection Between Darkness and Spiritual Growth.* New York: HarperCollins Publishers, 2004.

McCarty, Mary. *Loving: A Catholic Perspective on Vocational Lifestyle Choices.* Dubuque: Brown-Roa, 1993.

Merriam-Webster. "Virtue." http://www.merriam-webster.com/dictionary/virtue (accessed 20 May 2014).

Mother Teresa. *Come Be My Light: The Private Writings of the "Saint of Calcutta."* Edited by Brian Kolodiejchuk. New York: Doubleday, 2007.

*New American Bible Revised Edition.* 2011. http://new.usccb.org/bible/books-of-the-bible/index.cfm (accessed 29 June 2014).

Order of Carmelites. "What is Lectio Divina." http://ocarm.org/en/content/lectio/what-lectio-divina (accessed 27 May 2014).

Our Sunday Visitor Curriculum Division. *Course 1: The Word.* Huntington: Our Sunday Visitor, 2010.

_____. *Course 2: Son of the Living God.* Huntington: Our Sunday Visitor, 2011.

PBS. "This Emotional Life: Understanding Forgiveness." http://www.pbs.org/thisemotionallife/topic/forgiveness/understanding-forgiveness (accessed 20 March 2014).

Peck, M. Scott. *The Road Less Traveled.* New York: Simon and Schuster, 1978.

Pope Paul VI. *Evangelii Nuntiandi* (On Evangelization in the Modern World), 1975. http://www.vatican.va/holy_father/paul_vi/apost_exhortations/documents/hf _p-vi_exh_19751208_evangelii-nuntiandi_en.html (accessed 29 June 2014).

Rohr, Richard. "Daily Meditation: Transformative Dying: Collapsing into the Larger Life," April 14, 2014. http://myemail.constantcontact.com/Richard-Rohr-s-Meditation--Collapsing-into-the-Larger-Life.html?soid=1103098668616&aid=SZvXjpOEWkU (accessed 23 April 2014).

Rolheiser, Ronald. *The Holy Longing: The Search for a Christian Spirituality.* New York: The Doubleday Religious Publishing Group, Kindle Edition, 2014.

Rubin, Gretchen. *The Happiness Project: Or, Why I Spent a Year Trying to Sing in the Morning, Clean My Closets, Fight Right, Read Aristotle, and Generally Have More Fun.* Harper Collins, Inc.. Kindle Edition, 2009.

Ruffling, Janet. "Resisting the Demons of Busyness," *Spiritual Life.* Summer 1995: 79-89.

Schaper, Donna. *Sabbath Sense: A Spiritual Antidote for the Overworked.* Philadelphia: Innisfree Press, 1997.

Second Vatican Council. *Gaudium et Spes. Pastoral Constitution on the Church in the Modern World.* 7 Dec. 1965. Edited by Austin Flannery. Northport: Costello Publishing Co., 1996.

_____. *Lumen Gentium. Dogmatic Constitution of the Church.* 21 Nov. 1964. Edited by Austin Flannery. Northport: Costello Publishing Co., 1996.

Strong, James. *Strongest of Strong's Exhaustive Concordance of the Bible.* Grand Rapids: Zondervan, 2001

Think Exist. Quotation: "There is a God Shaped Vacuum in the Heart." http://thinkexist.com/quotation/there_is_a_god_shaped_vacuum_in_the_heart _of/166425.html (accessed 22 June 2014).

United States Conference of Catholic Bishops. "Archbishop Oscar Romero Prayer: A Step Along the Way" by Bishop Ken Untener. http://www.usccb.org/prayer-and-worship/prayers-and-devotions/prayers/archbishop_romero_prayer.cfm (accessed June 20, 2014).

_____. "Disciples Called to Witness: Part II," A statement by the Committee on Evangelization and Catechesis. Washington DC: United States Catholic

Conference, 2012. http://www.usccb.org/beliefs-and-teachings/how-we-teach/new-evangelization/disciples-called-to-witness/disciples-called-to-witness-part-ii.cfm (accessed 29 June 2014).

_____. "To Be a Christian Steward: A Summary of the U.S. Bishops' Pastoral Letter on Stewardship." Washington DC: United States Catholic Conference, 1992. http://www.usccb.org/beliefs-and-teachings/what-we-believe/stewardship/index.cfm (accessed 20 June 2014).

_____. *Brothers And Sisters To Us: Pastoral Letter on Racism.* Washington DC: United States Catholic Conference, 1979. http://www.usccb.org/issues-and-action/cultural-diversity/african-american/brothers-and-sisters-to-us.cfm (accessed 31 May 2014).

_____. *General Directory for Catechesis.* Washington DC: United States Catholic Conference, 1997.

_____. *Sharing Catholic Social Teaching: Challenges and Directions.* Washington DC: United States Catholic Conference, 1998. http://www.usccb.org/beliefs-and-teachings/what-we-believe/catholic-social-teaching/sharing-catholic-social-teaching-challenges-and-directions.cfm (accessed 29 June 2014).

_____. *United States Catholic Catechism for Adults.* Washington DC: United States Conference of Catholic Bishops, Kindle Edition, 2012.

West, Christopher. *Theology of the Body Explained: A Commentary on John Paul II's Man and Woman He Created Them.* Boston: Pauline Books, 2007.

Wicks, Robert. *Availability: The Spiritual Gift of Helping Others.* New York: The Crossroad Publishing Company, 1986.

_____. *Touching the Holy: Ordinariness, Self-Esteem and Friendship.* Notre Dame: Ave Maria Press, 1992.

Wink, Walter. *The Powers That Be.* Doubleday, 1998. http://www.cpt.org/files/BN%20-%20Jesus'%20Third%20Way.pdf (accessed 20 March 2014).

Wooden, Cindy. "Pope says Christians Should Have Restless Hearts Like St. Augustine's" *Catholic News Service*, August 28, 2013. Accessed June 23, 2014. http://www.catholicnews.com/data/stories/cns/1303694.htm.

World Synod of Catholic Bishops. *Justicia in Mundo* (Justice in the World). 1971. http://www.cctwincities.org/document.doc?id=69 (accessed 27 June 2014).

Made in the USA
Coppell, TX
02 August 2022

80754206R00081